About the author

I am a simple person with a complicated past, an outgoing individual buried under the waves of shyness, a human being that is kind to others and ruthless to one-self, a responsible adult with childlike playfulness, a loner screaming for affection, and my own worst critic.

Disclaimer

This book deals with a sensitive issue, and it includes mental struggle and physical illness that were, arguably, not always handled in the best way. I am, by no means, in a position to give specific pieces of medical advice, so this book should not be used for this purpose.

PUSSIFIED
A SEX CHANGE STORY I DIDN'T HAVE THE BALLS
TO TELL

INA FERENČIĆ

PUSSIFIED
A SEX CHANGE STORY I DIDN'T HAVE THE BALLS TO TELL

Vanguard Press

VANGUARD PAPERBACK

© Copyright 2022
Ina Ferenčić

The right of Ina Ferenčić
to be identified as author of
this work has been asserted by her in accordance with the
Copyright, Designs and Patents Act 1988.

A CIP catalogue record for this title is
available from the British Library.

ISBN 978 1 80016 318 8

*Vanguard Press is an imprint of
Pegasus Elliot MacKenzie Publishers Ltd.*
www.pegasuspublishers.com

First Published in 2022

**Vanguard Press
Sheraton House Castle Park
Cambridge England**

Printed & Bound in Great Britain

Dedication

This book is dedicated to my family and friends, to my late mother, who fought my wars for me and with me, and to everyone who seeks the same freedom these pages gave me.

Acknowledgements

I thank my dear childhood friend for proofreading my book and big *"thank you"* to every single person who helped me with feedback during the writing process.

Introduction

I have never been my biggest fan. Moreover, I always thought, if a personality of an individual is a drug and the other people that love them feel like they need an occasional feel-good dose of their presence, in my eyes, one hit of myself was too much for anybody. I felt nobody wanted to experience me again for some time, and if the case seemed opposite, in my mind, it was only because those people felt obligated to be nice. After all, we have known each other for years.

So why did I consider myself toxic and unworthy? Why did I feel people should leave me wanting less? That's a long story, and I am about to share it with you.

To be honest, I was not even sure if I should write the first two sentences in this paragraph in the past tense since I am not fully over the feelings that have been embedded deep inside of me since my teenage years. But since I feel like I am taking steps in a positive direction, hence this written work, I choose to take a sip of the half-full glass in this introduction.

I decided to be a straight shooter from the very first page, as I have no time or interest in dancing around this subject any more. I danced so hard my feet hurt more than my feelings or ego ever had. Avoidance has been my coping mechanism ever since I can remember, and the stressor was everything that I had identified as too hard to handle or uncomfortable.

So let's cut to the chase.

The world considers me a girl now, but I was born a boy, a sick child with a disorder of sex development/gender differentiation. As a result of that, I had sex change surgery at the age of six.

Was that my choice? No, but it was a choice my parents were confronted with, and there was nothing else to do. The medical condition was problematic enough for them to make a radical move that there was no coming back from. They decided that they would rather watch their child live and grow than mourn over a kid because of a decision they refused to make. They knew that if multiple reputable experts in medicine are telling you something that can make a difference between life and death, you better perk up your ears and listen.

Unclassified

It feels silly to give myself any label because I never wanted to place myself in any of the boxes. I don't personally know any other individual that went through something similar. I know they are out there, I just haven't looked hard enough, so I don't know anybody I can relate to.

If you are thinking to yourself right now, *Well, wait a minute, there are plenty of people who've decided to go through sex change surgery...* I will stop you right there because the difference is they chose to go under the knife, and I didn't.

There is no short version of my story, so answering seemingly simple questions can be very hard and frustrating. What approach to take and which words to choose is a million-dollar question for me. I have always considered myself "a girl who used to be a boy," but I do realize that everything is open to debate. All of this depends on your perspective.

How so? Well, if you look at my birth certificate, my ID, and all of my documents, in the eyes of the law, I am a female and have been one since 1994. But if you take a look from a biological standpoint, you cannot argue with the chromosomes, no matter how screwed up one small but significant part of my DNA is.

In a medical sense, I had an error. Think of it as a "blue screen of death" most of us have witnessed at one point or another on a Windows PC. My system was compromised and had reached a point where it could no longer operate safely. Yet, I was restored and rebooted. The new software they imagined I would have was glitchy, though, and it didn't exactly fit, but at least I was up and running, with or without bugs.

Your System Has Run into a Problem and Needs to Restart

Soon after I was born in 1988 in Croatia, doctors realized there was something wrong with me. This little boy, Ivan, named after his father, had something that had to be identified by examining the chromosomes in a blood sample — mixed gonadal dysgenesis.

Chromosome 45 was marked X, while chromosome 46 had an XY to its name. Since these cells typically have the XX or XY combination, you can see where the problem occurred during DNA replication and cell division. One Y drove off the road on Forty-fifth Street right into a brick wall, and since our cells, even the broken ones, multiply over and over again... well, good luck embryo, good luck fetus, and good luck baby. That particular Y is missing, so get ready for the potential negative effects on physical height, hormonal balance, and gonadal development.

Just as promised, I was struck with almost everything that such a medical condition predicts. My cognitive abilities were not impaired, but that was predictable since those are usually left perfectly untouched with this abnormality. All the other things a person with this prognosis could fear, though, were there.

Sealed Fate

Yes, at one point in time, there were some tiny balls, and, yes, there were traces of a penis. But those poor bastards stood no chance.

"We strongly recommend sex change surgery and that you continue raising your child, in a female sense."

Those are the words that put the stamp on it. Signed, sealed, and delivered. My parents said yes, and the surgeon eventually said, "Scalpel, please."

But I will not take you to the surgery and my new life just yet. There are plenty of things to share before the six-year-old me had to come to grips with the new reality.

In this book, I will reveal my life story, which will mean that you, the reader, will know more about me than anybody else up until this point. I will also give my opinion on various psychological issues that come in this kind of package, with the hope that this could help many people, including parents who find themselves in the same boat as mine did many years ago.

Life has dealt me plenty of shit and made me look for a shovel. I am not exactly sure, but I think I finally found one big enough. Now I can look at all the crap from a more positive standpoint and realize that this kind of shit can make stuff grow. Better stuff, called life lessons. So strap on, prepare yourself, because at the end of this book, you might just ask yourself, "What keeps this person going?"

Does that thought reek of depression? I understand why you might get that impression but hear me out and try to understand me. After all, I did wake up from the operation at the age of six, and I gave myself a new name. My parents didn't have to debate about that because I did the work for them. I will go through that in more detail in a later chapter, too.

So as you can see, I had plenty on my plate from an early age. That's why I will take you through the whole timeline, from early childhood and teen years to adulthood, where I lost my mother and moved to Zagreb — the very city that chillingly shined through my hospital window blinds every time the night arrived.

I will share with you my memories and feelings before and after the surgery. I will also reveal the challenges I had to face in school, in a small town where stories like this tended to spread like wildfire. I will tell you about shameful encounters, awkward moments that made me wish I could end everything right there, and I will also reflect on most of it from the perspective of a grown-up.

As I am writing this, I am thirty-three years old — twenty-seven years removed from the semi-body-altering procedure. Notice I mentioned body, not the mind.

The Driving Force

What potential do I see in this book, and what are my expectations?

Well, from a reader's perspective, I hope for an interesting read and encounter with a few useful and valuable nuggets of wisdom. From my perspective, this is the diary I have never written, the courage I have never displayed, and the memories that should be externally stored to stay accurate and vivid. There are plenty of things I remember that could just vanish from my brain in five or ten years or be distorted.

Think of it as memory insurance, as a personal challenge, as a project, and a cry for freedom. The shackles are coming off.

Besides sharing my story with you, the main objective of this book is to lead you through my life's chapters with straightforward, digestible, easy to read, yet interesting content. Please, don't mistake me for somebody who thinks his or her life is so special that it should be written out with a golden pen. This is the first time I will be discussing my issues out loud, and outside my head, so I hope these pages will not be interpreted as one giant sob story.

I am just pouring my heart out to anyone who concludes that this might be an engrossing read, as I think there are some lessons I learned the hard way, that are good and valuable enough to be shared.

The first chapters have their focus on my life before the operation. They are not the longest chapters in the world, I'll admit it, but since this is not fiction and I have no interest in making things up, these paragraphs are limited to my brain's ability to hold on to some pretty distant memories.

The later chapters, which revolve around the medical procedure itself, depict more vivid stuff from my head, and more recent stories can be found in the final segment.

When I was a kid, one piece of leaked information from my life was enough for others to ask questions or even look at me as a freak. So I thought to myself, maybe in the land of grown-ups, the same story could be just as intriguing, only this time, all of its lessons will be used productively.

So if you are ready, I am, too.

Before you continue, I need to emphasize one important thing. In the upcoming chapters, you might get the feeling that some relevant details about my condition are missing, and you may wish to learn more. If that ends up being the case, the third-to-last part of this book, called "Technical Specification", could be just enough to fill in the blanks. This is the text that was written with the help of my first doctor, and I separated it so the rest of the book would be lighter.

With that being said, let's begin.

Chapter 1: Cut and Dried

Once upon a time, there was a humble young woman from a tiny town in central Croatia, the very place I spent my entire childhood in. That loving, happy-go-lucky, witty, photogenic, no-make-up-wearing gal, my mom, fell for my dad — the minute she saw him walking into a coffee shop.

There he was, arriving at the place like a boss. He had a thick beard, he was tall, he was handsome, he was confident, he was charming, and he was broken. Not in spirit — he was on crutches.

This cool, calm, and collected guy was selected by my mother, the feelings were mutual, and before those bones managed to heal up, they were in a relationship.

Everything was going in the right direction. They got married and had their first kid, my sister, in 1984. Things were fine, life was pretty close to ideal, their parents were still around, they had many friends, they both had jobs they were happy with, and they had enough money for them not to be concerned or stressed by their finances.

The thing is, life will not let you simply enjoy it that easily and for that long. It's not like my parents lived in luxury or at the expense of others, so the "great equalizer" had to arrive, but I guess everything seemed too ideal for this steady curve on a life chart to continue to ascend. That's just the way it is sometimes — what comes up must come down at some point.

There were no indications of what was about to happen to one current and one future member of the family. And who would've ever seen this one coming?

You are in your late thirties, you are at your life's peak, with one healthy kid behind you and another one on the way, and the next thing you know, you are faced with your child's mortality, along with your own. Since this is happening at approximately the same time, you are forced to neglect yourself, take your mind off your own troubles, and dedicate the precious energy you have to a kid who got confronted with adversity way too early in life.

In normal circumstances, this is simply not something a person is preparing for. It's not like saving money for rainy days, where you know that financial problems can be fixed with a stash of cash. Life's adversities, where health is concerned, have an outcome that is affected by the things that are usually unmoved by the dollar. The procedure on its own did not directly cost anything, and the only thing you can rely on in this situation is the medical team's competence, the strength of the patient, and the weakness of the illness. If the expertise is poor, the will of the patient is weak, and the strength of the illness is substantial, the chances are no amount of money will be sufficient.

No Health, No Wealth

Four and a half years after my sister was born, I stormed into this world, and all of a sudden, things got complicated for my family.

Congratulations, it is a boy, and oh boy, did the future seem bright for me for a minute. The financial stability of the parents was there, the genes were apparently there, and amazing family support of our small group was present, too.

But what in the world do you have if you don't have your health?

Instead of me growing up to my full potential, life handed our family an ill child, and instead of my mother staying healthy and working at her job for twenty-plus years, she ended up with kidney failure. She was sentenced to life on dialysis, which ended up lasting heroic and above average, but still way too short, twenty years.

Her retirement began before she was even able to enjoy her job properly, and her entire life from then on was a steep downhill, health-wise.

As you might imagine, there was a shitload of dilemmas in our household when the final incision-decision was about to be made about me. Even though the choice was obvious, it was not an easy one to make. But since getting cancer was a strong possibility in a scenario where endocrinologists' and surgeons' words were ignored, sex reassignment surgery was inevitable.

Let's face it, no reputable expert would advocate for that solution based on a flip of a coin, so my parents pretty much had a no-brainer placed in front of them.

But while they had to do what they had to do, the date was more flexible. In the end, the chosen age was six, and it was approximately one year away from my first grade.

The mind was made up. It was over. It was done. I had to change before school, and I wish I was talking about my pants.

Trained, But Not Rewired

Make no mistake about me. Even though my development as a boy was not comparable to a male child that had no medical issues, I was still an XY. No question about it. Short hair? Check! Rough-and-tumble messing around and horseplay with the boys? Check! A boy-ish voice in the beginning? Check that one off the list, too.

So, the journey after that surgery was never meant to be easy for me. I'm pretty sure that everybody was aware of that, but between them and me, only I would know the extent of the issues. That would still be the case even if I was completely open about everything that was troubling me before, during, and after my teens. But in reality, I was as closed as a government building on Labor Day.

That's why I don't have any desire to blame anyone for my troubles. I simply don't have any grounds to do it on. You can create make-believe grounds and pretend like you are actually standing on something solid, that's true, but channeling the blame and guilt-trips will ultimately lead you to an even greater hole. Not only will you realize that, in the end, nothing is fixed, but you will also feel the ricochet of all those bullets you so willingly sent off flying earlier.

While I was collected enough not to point fingers, I failed to realize just how much of my existence is dedicated to avoiding the subject. And with the way my friends are reacting to my confession now, I can describe my earlier approach as the main mistake of my life. A mistake that, hopefully, many young people will avoid in time.

When I opened my notebook with the intention to scribble out ideas and main points for this book, I had to dig deep into my memory to give some depth to my story. Luckily, I have no issues with remembering the most important parts, and from now on, because of these pages, these recollections have become indestructible.

Memory Bank

So many grown-ups say this: I had the best childhood one can possibly have! But I really do think I had a childhood that any kid would be jealous of, and I'm being completely honest with you. Non-stop play, maximum freedom, plenty of fun, adventure, and mud, and, luckily, minimum-to-no blood.

My feelings are strong on this one. I am sticking to the notion that everything was close to perfect back then, yet I do have flashes of scenes that had the potential to overshadow these beautiful, idealistic, and nostalgic views of my earliest days.

Imagine other kids looking through their window and seeing a yard they are about to play in, a swing they are about to swing on, or friends they are about to run around with. And now imagine me looking at the window and seeing the damn buildings of Zagreb and shining lights in the distance.

I was a hundred kilometers away from my little town, away from my family and friends, and I remember looking at those concrete structures and thinking how cold those lives must be compared to the paradise that awaited me at home, the place packed with green yards and family houses.

I didn't want to be in Zagreb, yet things were out of my control. Hospital time gradually increased, so from time to time, they sent me home on weekends, and I traveled back to Zagreb on weekdays. This way, everything was a tad easier. Some children in that hospital had no such luxury, either because they were too far away, too sick, or their parents just couldn't afford frequent trips back and forth.

So, I guess my family and friends did one hell of a job of keeping me content, fulfilled, and sane, and because of that, all of my positive childhood memories are actually a feather in their cap. They were the straw I was holding on to every time life got tough in Croatia's capital. Those familiar faces were, I guess, on my mind every time it seemed like my mind couldn't take it any more.

I had two realities. One was a place of sanctuary; the other one was the upside-down world, where stranger things were happening every day. So I would conclude this is one of the reasons I haven't lost my marbles.

Mama's Boy

I'm sure you've all seen children super-glued to their parents' legs in uncomfortable situations. I wasn't one of those kids exactly, but I did develop a stronger bond with my mother. This was, I'm sure you would agree, something to be expected considering the circumstances. My mother was by my side throughout most of my life's adversities.

But during my long hospital stays, something happened that wasn't expected back then, but it is obvious in hindsight — I adopted my new routines and everything that came along with them.

It's amazing and terrifying to realize what kind of stuff people can get used to. I had no interest in making new friends or getting familiar with the hospital, yet it still happened on several occasions. Every time that happened, I felt like I downgraded.

This reminds me of the consequences that can derive from a financial situation a lot of people find themselves in.

You have a certain income, you are stretching it, but managing to live a normal life, and you are good. But now, suddenly, you find yourself in a position where you receive less money, and while it seems impossible at first glance, you still manage to adapt, and you realize that, in the end, not much has changed.

Then you think to yourself, *If everything is the same right now, why in the world didn't I live this life when I had more money, because I could've saved that extra cash every month.*

It's OK to think that way, but the fact that we continue to adapt to lesser things bothers me. People keep sliding that bar down, and they learn to live with slightly worse conditions all the time. We settle for less every time "less" becomes normal.

To me, the hospital was a downgrade of my life, and I had no desire to adapt. It would be like admitting that this place with colorful walls and playrooms is not all that bad. But man, time gets you in the end. If you encounter something often enough, a "familiar" will pop out of almost any situation. But that was still settling for less, and I didn't like it.

As far as me being a clingy child, I can admit it to an extent, but that manifested only in one small part of my childhood and not in some dramatic super-glue way.

What I was, and still partially am, is socially disorientated. My social equilibrium is out of whack, punched out like I was in a boxing match, and only recently have I felt like I can actually differentiate life phases and recognize if my life is moving, spinning, or standing still.

Later we will see if I'll go full circle with this boxing analogy and end up being punch-drunk in twenty-plus years. There are so many hits you can take, but I am optimistic since I've learned how to roll with the punches.

A lot of moving parts, some of which are somewhat unrelated, played a part in building me as a person.

So, why was I more or less OK with staying at the hospital as a five-year-old, before the surgery happened? Maybe Ivan had something to do with that, and I am not referring to myself.

Big Bro Figure

Most of us need to be a pretty tough cookie to successfully cruise through this existence; that's simply one of life's requirements if you want to survive the rough seas with minimum-to-no consequences. This is where the support system comes in, and we all know how important it is to have encouraging and caring people around who can help you avoid being crumbled.

But when you are a kid, the support system is all you can rely on, as you are too small to even comprehend the severity of any problem. As a child, you are ignorant and innocent, and that's the way it should be.

As far as I am concerned, my first make-or-break challenge appeared when I was five and a half years old, during my pre-operation hospital stays. And when my supportive family members were not physically there, I had to improvise and find some other center of gravity.

This is where one boy comes into the picture. He was my roommate; he was at least five or six years older than me; we shared the same name, and he was the one that made me feel like I had somebody to turn to when my parents were not around.

For a child, to be open and approachable is not easy when you are among a bunch of strangers in a cold, sterile environment filled with sadness and desperation. So you keep grabbing the straws, and you identify any traces of warmth as a potential sanctuary.

But as we will see later, then you proceed to settle in, and it suddenly becomes too hard to separate and too tough to look for another port in the storm.

I don't remember too much about Ivan, and I am not sure what illness he had, but I know he was somebody I found comfort in. Now, when I rewind the remaining traces of the tape of those early memories, and I think about it, I cannot actually be certain that this person is alive and well today. If he is, he is in his late thirties, and there is a small chance that he could actually remember me.

Why did he stay fixed in my memory even though twenty-eight years have passed since I last saw him?

I recollect going to sleep in the bed on the left side of the room and him being on the opposite side, and we would watch each other and talk to each other as it was the only way I could sink into a dream state.

That really stuck with me because, let's face it, there's a really good chance you are a kind, humble, well-behaved, and thoughtful kid if you are ten, eleven, or twelve years old, and you find it within you to offer comfort to a clingy five-year-old you don't even know.

But that's what he did. He talked to me before I went to sleep, and if I remember correctly, he once visited me to wish me luck when I was strapped to an IV while waiting for doctors to come and roll me away to whatever place I needed to be taken to. I don't remember what procedure that was, but I do remember the preps for it and a few kids saying hello to me as they were passing by.

So why do I wonder if Ivan is alive today? Because I saw him unconscious as he was being rushed in.

I remember it so clearly. It was evening, I was in the waiting room, a place where toys were scattered all over the floor for kids to play with, and the elevator door suddenly opened. I was just standing there, and there was Ivan, unconscious, on a rolling bed, being rushed towards the hallway. He didn't move at all, and I distinctly recollect a redness on his slightly darker-colored face.

To this day, I don't know what happened to him and why he was at the hospital in the first place. But I'm guessing, and maybe I'm speaking nonsense now, that he was a diabetic and he fell into a diabetic coma. This is my best guess, and I still wonder whether he is alive and well today.

The event is too far away, and the timeline is too blurry for me to be able to figure out if I ever saw him again after he lost consciousness. I really hope I did, but the only thing I can do is assume. All I know is I liked his company very much, and I wish I could remember more details about this period of my life.

He was not the only person in that hospital who I followed like a lost puppy. If Ivan was a brother figure, one particular nurse was a mother figure in my eyes because I was her annoying little shadow. If you wanted to find me, you just had to find her because I was more often than not in her vicinity.

I remember her being very nice, but that would be a logical characterization even if I didn't remember any details about that woman. That's simply because my mom set the bar too high for any poor "mother figure" to hit my radar.

I've got to admit, I was a cute kid. I was a cute, well-behaved child who was also in a lot of trouble, so no wonder this triggered people's instinct to protect me. All of them did that from the goodness of their hearts, so as much as I hate hospitals, it would be disingenuous on my part to deny that those healthcare institutions had some of the best people I've ever met.

So Ivan, my namesake buddy, I thank you for your kindness, wherever you are.

White Hospital Lies

People love you, and sometimes people lie to you on a small scale because of that love. It would sound contradictory if we never witnessed and practiced innocent, well-intentioned lies, but we all know them pretty well since we hear them first, and maybe the most, in early childhood.

I don't know what it's like to be a parent, but I'm sure a bunch of people pre-set many of the same goals as they are about to become a mother or a father. One of the important aims, I assume, is maximum honesty. In other words, parents vow to lie to their children as little as possible.

Zero bullshitting stands a zero chance, of course, and that's where harmless white lies enter the frame. My mom sometimes didn't have a choice, but she kept those little trivial untruths to a minimum.

I remember one particular visit to the hospital. My mother arrived during visiting hours. This time her cousin was with her. I don't know how long their visit

31

lasted, but their leaving on that particular day was something that, for some reason, stayed quite vivid in my memory. It's one of those recollections where you know exactly which people were standing where, and you remember most of what was said and the vibe of the entire scene.

Visiting time was over, and I was aware of that. But on that day, I simply wasn't in the mood to be left behind, despite the fact that this had already become the routine. But because of the fact that it was the routine, I knew the drill, and I expected them to leave any minute.

So instead of throwing a fit, which is something I never had a habit of doing, I had my questions ready. And just as I had my material prepared, my mother had all the answers ready to be presented at a moment's notice.

"Why do you have to go now? Where are you going? Will you still return today before driving home?"

Bang, bang, bang, I fired every bullet I had. But my mom was ready. She told me how she needed to take the car to the auto shop because the tires needed to be changed on our Yugo. Yes, we had a Yugo, a white one, brand new, imported from Germany. Now finish laughing, and let's continue with the story.

Did my mom return that day? No, but I didn't expect her to, as she never gave me any false hopes, which is really important.

Imagine telling your hospitalized child you will return in fifteen minutes, just so the kid would stop crying, and then you drive off home while hoping little guy or little girl got distracted by nurses and toys and forgot all about your promise. It sounds bad and even cruel, but some parents do exactly that, out of desperation, while at the same time, the described activity is ripping their hearts apart.

Hospitals are places filled with strange energy and distinctive smells. Even the people who only visit someone there for thirty minutes notice this.

I can tell you first hand they are very unusual places. On the one hand, hospitals save human lives. A person can enter the building all beaten up, bloodied up, cut open, or unconscious, and that same person can exit this healthcare institution all healed up and brand new.

On the flip side, these are the locations where bad diagnoses turn worse, where last words are spoken, where parents watch their children suffer and vice versa.

Everyone agrees that health is the most important thing, and every person in a hospital, from patients and family members and friends who visit, to specialized medical and nursing staff who walk up and down the hallways, have nothing but health issues on their minds.

It doesn't feel fair to call hospitals dark, depressing places, but they can certainly seem that way.

So what's a little white lie if it spares a hospitalized child even more pain?

As I see it, this is a balancing act for most moms and dads. On one side, you have the option of absolute truth, which often seems cruel and cold even though you do it with the assumption that this will, in the end, benefit your child. On the other hand, you can lie through your teeth for temporary pain relief and suffer later as you struggle with guilt while your kid faces the truth in isolation. Small kids won't go into some deep analysis about the potential benefits and repercussions of the lie, but what they do know is they don't like or appreciate being tricked and deceived.

Being a parent — is there a more complicated job in the world? You have to run, juggle, duck, dive, entertain, and console. You are a guardian, a therapist, a friend, a hero, and a figure of admiration to your kid.

Bawling Uncontrollably

How do you cope with emotional pain? How often do you cry alone, and how often do you do the same in front of other people? I would like to get readers' feedback on this because I am curious if my "straight face" approach to life's difficulties is a common thing. Feel free to send me an e-mail about this.

If you see hidden tears as a big mistake, I'm afraid I don't have much to brag about. I'm not exactly a role model as far as dealing with emotions is concerned.

My default life emojis mostly have silly faces and confused facial expressions on them, with a couple of smileys in between. Little frowny icons are not as common, but when they come, they usually have desperation on their face or blue, teary streams under their eyes and over their cheeks.

In my life, during these thirty-three years, I've only cried four times in someone else's presence, and on two of those occasions, my mom was the only person around.

The first time this happened I was actually pretending I had the sniffles to get my mother to ask me, "What's wrong?" My goal was to tell her there was a chance I could receive a bad grade on an exam, but I didn't have the guts to initiate this topic. When she finally asked me what was wrong, the unexpected happened — I actually did start crying for real and out of control.

She told me everything would be OK no matter what, and guess what — the next day, I got a B on that very exam. Just for reference, I was ten years old then, but the attachment I had to my parents was more comparable to that of a five-year-old. I was falling far behind on that front.

The other tear-dam broke in a similar time frame, but on this occasion, pain was the straw that broke the camel's back. I had to go through a certain procedure more than twenty times in four years, all without anesthesia, and on one occasion, the pain was so unbearable that I exited the room in tears, and I walked towards my mom as she approached me to give me a hug. I tried so hard but was unable to hold my tears back.

I will talk about these procedures in greater detail later on.

I've cried fifteen or twenty times in my life, but in a vacuum. Too often, I fought that lump in the throat, which happens to be muscle tension as your glottis is trying to stay open but gets forced close every time you swallow. (I just googled that!)

I also found out that crying as a coping mechanism was possibly formed as a sign of submission, as it would be more likely that an attacker would spare the life of a whiny victim.

It's one of the theories, but who knows, maybe that's the reason I'm fighting it. Maybe I'm rebelling against ancient genes as I don't like the feeling of being vulnerable. Maybe I would rather get beaten to death than stay alive because of the mercy of others.

Maybe it's just a guy thing.

I can tell you this, though — no sane person will think another person's tears are shameful. So if you feel like crying your heart out, do it and give it absolutely all you've got. Ignore the theory mentioned above.

Crying is a social thing, a social cue to people around you, a sign that they should give you a hug, care, and attention. And in the opposite scenario, you should give your attention to others when tears are streaming down their faces. So react, give, and you shall receive. This is solid advice I just presented, but the irony is that many of you are probably more ready to put it into practice than me. Still, to this day, I would rather suffer through on my own, as I feel others have their own issues to deal with. My first instinct is to avoid being a nuisance, but I did make some progress with this. Being a bit more open, as it turns out, makes things a lot easier.

It seems like I am stating the obvious; it probably is a "duh" thing to say, but because of that, it's really a great shame that so many people hold their stuff in or leave the most important stuff out while interacting with others. We know what we should do; we just fail to practice it.

The Cancer Issue

There were plenty of things to cry about, yet I forced my tears back into my eye sockets on a regular basis. But often, I didn't feel any sadness, even though the circumstances gave justification for that.

Instead of being sad, I was open and curious, which is something I lost in my teens and regained in my early thirties. I was six and seven years old when I asked questions that I didn't have answers to, and I answered plenty of other people's inquiries. I wasn't afraid or ashamed.

For many reasons, I lost this ability two or three years later, and it took me more than twenty years to find the fraction of courage I once had.

I know my mom didn't have it easy, but boy, my curiosity must've been tough to deal with sometimes. As a matter of fact, if she were around today, I would ask her how she felt when I came forward with one particular question concerning my health. This was a good example of the openness I mentioned I once possessed.

I was six years old, I was very aware of the circumstances surrounding my case, as were my friends, too. Some of them were more curious than others, and they had questions.

On one particularly hot topic, I couldn't satisfy the inquisitive minds of my buddies with an answer, so I forwarded the dilemma to my mom, the only person who could help us resolve it. And of all the times, I decided to satisfy this curiosity in the middle of the night.

Don't ask me why, because I don't have a clue, but I bet you that I fell asleep right after that, and my mother didn't.

A few of my friends knew about the cancer thing, but we weren't sure if I had already got it or whether I would get it if no surgery was performed. You know, it was something every pre-school child is normally debating. But hey, they asked, and I had to find out, so that night I woke my mom up to ask her this question:

"Mom, do I already have cancer, or did the doctor say I will get it if no surgery is performed?"

What in the world I was thinking, I don't know, but despite the delicate nature of the question and the person asking it, there was no silence in between me talking, and my mother responding.

"The cancer could come if no surgery is performed," she answered.

I just said OK, and I felt content as I had everything cleared up. As far as my mom is concerned, I don't know how she reacted internally, but I guess she was confident she was doing the right thing.

And she knew me well because she was absolutely right.

That's the difference between my younger self and my teenage self, and I guess my mom was the factor that made all the difference.

While she was in control, everything was fine, things were discussed when needed, and no stone was left unturned. But when responsibility started to slowly shift from her to my teenage self, it turned out I was not prepared for at least part of the incoming problems. I managed to figure out a lot of stuff; it just took some time and some battlefield damage for me to get here.

Looking back at everything now, it was the right thing to do, to let me be and to give me more freedom.

It was my responsibility to report any major problems on my journey. The fact that I was pretending everything was OK when that was not the case… well, that one is on me.

If someone doesn't know about your troubles, that person may not be able to help you. So silence is not the solution if you crave some guidance, advice, and attention from the people around you, and straight-out lying and convincing others that everything is peachy is even worse. That's actually the biggest disservice you can do to yourself.

So now, let's finally talk about the procedure that made me out of him.

Chapter 2: Life-Changing/Saving/Ruining Surgery

As I mentioned before, I managed to get used to the hospital stays, and I even made some friends, even though this was never my intention. But the new circumstances didn't last because life is like this: just when you feel you are finally getting comfortable with something, things flip on you. And I really got served this time.

It's over, little Ivan, time for you to change your very being. Not shoes, not a T-shirt, a hairstyle, or a toy — but yourself. Forget about the familiar environment and the kids with whom you shared your loneliness. Forget about the nice medical staff that you got used to seeing on a daily basis, and never mind those familiar hallways you were roaming through from one day to another out of boredom or curiosity. It's time for you to relocate.

Something's Fishy

You know shit is about to hit the fan when bedpans are about to become your reality for weeks to come.

A tiny old me was a simple child, but that little guy was not raised by a fool. I was aware something big was coming. I felt all those cumulative medical exams had to erupt in some manner. It all had to lead to something significant because many children were coming and going, and I was lying and staying.

It was an incredible feeling to see my mother every time she came to visit me, but damn it, I was genuinely getting pissed off by the fact I never got to leave for good. I've never felt the joy that comes close to the joyful emotions that overwhelmed me and filled me every time I saw my mother's smiling eyes after several days apart. At the same time, it's tough for me to describe the sorrow that I experienced every time those eyes aimed in the opposite direction as she walked away.

If I think about those moments hard enough, I can still feel the way I felt back then, for a split second. And there is one other thing I remember, too — desperation at one point became so prevalent that I simply thought to myself, *Let's get this over with already.*

The relocation was not significant if we merely talk about distance, but this was a new universe to me. I swear to you, and this may only be my bad orientation at fault, but it took me years to realize that my old hospital home and my new one, were just a few floors apart.

That should've been obvious to me because I walked and screamed my way across that line at the age of six, but I guess the horror played with my memory, and the connection wasn't there any more.

Uncharted Territory

Drama was truly never my thing, but I became a drama prince on one particular day. This act had everything. It was an edgy plot, filled with a range of intense emotions, physical displays, and loud vocals. I was not ready to change, but that didn't matter because I would never be prepared enough, so other people had to get me ready. And you bet your ass I turned into a fierce resistance fighter as a response.

What I'm about to tell you is a story that perfectly describes a person's opposition to change. My reaction, I think, was a raw display of emotions that many grown-ups feel but do not show due to the fact they are mature people.

In a situation where I was crying and resisting, an older person would walk the walk with the acceptance of what was about to come. But the manifestation of desperation would still be there nevertheless, only internally.

Who knows, maybe that's one of the reasons children are more likely to heal properly after a significant change. They don't seem to bottle up their feelings as much.

I will share with you the details about the beginning of the end of one major part of my life. When we talk about the line that gets crossed, in my case, it was represented by the hospital steps that led to another floor of the building. This was the floor where surgeries were carefully planned, and, somehow, I knew that when I crossed that line, everything would irreversibly change.

This is how much the situation escalated.

The main nurse from my old, familiar floor approached me, and she took me by the hand. This was not something she would usually do, so I started to move my fist in the opposite direction. As she held tighter, I resisted harder, and the situation turned into a tug-of-war. She was pretty tall, and she was strong, so I had no shot at escaping her grip. And as we approached the door that led to the previously mentioned stairs, I became more and more desperate.

We were getting closer and closer to the point of no return, so I cried more and more, and I pulled even harder. Again, with no success. I don't know if I was screaming because I was leaving the familiar place and entering into the unknown or if I actually mourned over the identity I was about to lose.

Whatever it was, I did try my best to avoid this fate, and my best was not good enough.

My heart and soul were weeping. My cries echoed through the hallways. I was helpless. Mother was not there to calm me down and hug me; nobody was there to save me. I might as well have been going to an execution, and in a way, I was. The clock was ticking as my old life was counting down its final days.

Poor little Ivan, he was so young.

Tragic Endings

The nurse that was dragging me towards my new environment managed to do so quite easily. She left me there, turned me over like some package to her colleagues, people I saw for the first time in my life. Suddenly I was surrounded by kids who, on average, were quite sicker than the girls and boys, downstairs.

While writing this book, I've been trying to remember any particular face from that new hospital room, but I can't. Maybe the main reason is the fact that most of these youngsters were strapped to their beds and connected to their IV lines. It was not easy to see their faces.

This was a whole new terrain. Roaming the hallways was something we would never do, and the only thing I knew about this floor was that it contained grown-ups five or six rooms away from us. This floor was the place where surgeries were planned, and just like the steel of a scalpel that is used to cut open human flesh during a procedure — the feeling was cold.

Nothing was familiar. There were no colorful walls or children's paintings, at least as far as I can remember.

There was nothing that could take your mind off the fact that you were in that situation. There was only the smell of the fruit the parents brought to their kids — damn bananas and clementines can still make me cringe today.

Also, the room I was in looked like a hospital version of an open-plan office. There were many beds, not just two like on that other floor. There was less privacy, and you could hear and see most of the happenings despite the fact that there was more space between fellow pre-teen patients.

Another important distinction from the old floor was the pace that led to the outcome of the situation. Everything was happening much quicker, which was kind of scary.

I wanted some conclusion, and I wanted to go home, but I didn't feel comfortable with the new dynamics. I don't remember having any days off — something was always happening. It was like a timer counting down to zero, with the effect of time seemingly flying faster as it approached that final point. You get anxious, and eventually, you receive that call.

Well, actually, when you are a kid, you don't receive any calls, your parents do. You, the kid, will most likely not be informed. One day they just stop giving you stuff to eat, they hook you up to an IV, and in the morning, the rolling bed pops up uninvited.

Suddenly, you are ordered to count from ten to zero, while something that looks like a cup from a jockstrap is being placed over your mouth.

The Final Cut

Looking back at it now, I am not entirely sure at which point the operation became one hundred percent inevitable. I did have a few more checkups before it happened, like an ultrasound exam while peeing on command. In the end, whatever that noninvasive medical exam showed, it wasn't something that changed anyone's mind.

Let's finally go to that operating room.

Keep in mind that this part is pieced together from several short snippets I managed to keep in my mind, as there is no longer a version of this event stored anywhere in my brain. I always wondered why I remember details after the surgery, yet I can barely recollect several frames of the moments before going under. Nevertheless, I'm glad I managed to hold on to anything.

What I do remember is feeling calm as they were wheeling me out. I'm not sure where that sense of peace came from, maybe they sprinkled something in my IV, but my state of mind was certainly not reflecting the actual situation. If it wasn't the drugs, the genuine care from the people around me could've been the place that soothing energy was coming from.

I can tell you from my experience that nurses can take your hand, tell you everything will be OK, and that gesture will really make an important difference. There are truly some special, compassionate human beings out there that have that ability, and if anyone should be doing such a mentally demanding job, it's them.

"So this is it, honey. We will just place this over your mouth. You will take a little nap, you will wake up, and all of this will be over."

"Ten… nine… eight…" Zzz.

Everything went black. My life was now in someone else's hands. Those long periods of examining and planning and weighing up the options — everything had been leading up to this.

How long did the operation last? I have no clue. But what was a second for me was probably days for my parents. In that second, tracks were changed mid-ride. My life was different now, and my parents' new job was to make sure that I didn't go off the rails.

Chapter 3: Goodnight, Ivan, Good Morning, Ina

I know very well what it's like to be a person in the hospital, waiting for something to happen as a defendant waits for a judicial decision. These are undoubtedly anxious moments, but you feel better if you are awarded one of the best lawyers you can get your hands on. So actually, my job in that chapter was done; sleeping was the easiest part of this whole experience. Experts who had my parents' trust had one mission — to justify that trust, and that implied I would physically be as close to female as possible.

The rest was up to me.

And they did their job pretty well, everyone agreed. The next move was mine, and it's pretty clear I'm still trying to figure out the game. But there was no delay — I had my first challenge shortly after opening my eyes.

Hi! My Name Is (What?)

I woke up from my deep sleep, and everything felt fine, just as the nurse promised. I experienced no pain; I was sleepy, dazed, yet relieved and peaceful. I knew what kind of operation this was, but I had no idea about the state I was in. I was lying down, my hand was tied to the bed so I would not mess up my IV while sleeping, and they strongly advised me to move as little as possible.

As soon as my mother was allowed, she was there beside me. My mom was the only person I wanted to see at that moment and, luckily, she was allowed to be there. Who knows what kind of reaction she expected from me and how it compared to my actual response, but I'm pretty sure she was not too surprised, as I was pretty prepared for this moment. She knew it because she prepared me.

I could tell quite a few stories about how smart my mother was, but only one is needed. Her brilliance lies in the fact that she carefully gave me all the right information about my condition. She knew me by heart, she knew what I could take, process and handle, and as a result of that, they all had minimum problems when the operation arrived.

Here's proof of that, and this is my favorite story. As a matter of fact, a few years ago I decided that I will think about this story at least a few times a year, so I don't forget any of the precious details. Not only do I want to preserve it, but I want to keep it intact, its original state — no facts excluded and no false information included.

Considering how memory is fragile and prone to destruction and inaccurate reconstruction, this is a necessary move. After all, my mom was the only person I discussed this with, and she is no longer here.

So because of all that, this short story you are about to read did not change in twenty-eight years. It's the same now as it was before.

I was on my back, not able to do anything other than stare at the ceiling and look left and right. The first family member I saw was my mother. She was looking at me. She leaned over me to stroke my hair. I felt like an angel was hovering over me, telling me the hardest parts were finally behind us. She had her sweet, soothing, comforting smile on her face, and she looked relieved.

After my mom confirmed I soldiered through the worst, she asked me the question I will remember forever, word by word.

"We need to give you a new name. What would you like to be called?"

There was no hesitation on my part. The question was expected, clear as day, and it took maybe two seconds for me to reply.

"Ina," I said.

This name was my first, and if I remember well, my only choice. That's because one of my best friend's name was Ina. She lived across the road from me, her parents still do, and for that relatively short time we knew each other, we became very close.

"OK, deal. Your name is Ina from now on," my mother replied.

That was official for me, and I was the one who made it that way. The name my friends know, the one that is printed on all of my documents and on the cover of this book, is the name I picked for myself.

We can all agreee that went well. Now imagine how everything had the potential to be drastically different.

My parents could've ignored the subject, avoided it, kept me out of the loop as a way of trying to shield me from any harm. They could've debated over a name for months and lied endlessly to me about the reasons I was in the hospital in the first place.

Instead of that — and ninety-nine percent of the credit for this goes to my mother — I was up to date and informed, and I knew that the answer to my mother's question was not child's play. I was aware that the reply I gave her was the reply that was going to be taken into account.

I don't know how this managed to play out, and it still intrigues me to this day. I look at six-year-olds now as a grown-up, and I realize there is not much responsibility you can give them unless it's choosing what kind of sandwich they would like to have or what cartoon they would like to watch next. If you ask them to choose their clothes for the day, don't expect them to color coordinate the outfit, and they will probably not check the weather outside to see if they need something extra on top of their favorite T-shirt.

That is normal; kids are kids, and I was the same in almost every scenario. But in this case, I had to, I guess, gain a few years. I had to be mature for a little while because serious questions demanded serious answers.

So this is it; this is how I got my name.

The name Ina is actually the name of a Croatian oil company, so many people over the years joked about that. People who don't know me often ask me how I got that name, and up until now, I wouldn't give a reply to that question. I knew, if I explained, they would not believe me. And explaining further would be equal to opening one giant can of worms.

There is no way I can start explaining my story and then pull the brake and say, "So, this is it, in short." There is no short version; there's nothing brief I can say that would give all the info without pulling new questions along with it. So I just decided not to speak about it at all.

Now I have this book, so if you want to know more about me, you're in luck.

Re-Balancing Act

When you are tied to the bed, connected to an IV, away from your family and friends, and down in the dumps, there's nothing like a cold, stainless steel bedpan under your ass to brighten up your day. I don't care what the official name of that metallic shitter is — that bitch was never stainless again.

53

That period was probably the most depressing to me because my movements were restricted as we waited for my post-operative wounds to heal. I wish I knew how long that took, but this is another detail from my past that is blurry.

What I can tell you is that it was too long. I remember being sick and tired of hearing echos from outside without being able to walk there to check them out more closely. I hated the late evenings and the whole atmosphere of a dark room with light shining from the hallways because my old hospital floor had those lights dimmed. So when nature called, I had to aim eyes and ears in that direction because any shadow or a female voice meant I could call someone to bring me that infamous metallic object.

When you're lying down, how many days or weeks need to pass before you completely lose the ability to stay upright by yourself without falling flat on your face? I could use that info to try to figure out the minimum amount of time I spent in that bed because I passed the point where your inner ear goes berserk. Two or three weeks is my guess.

When they concluded I could get up, I thought I would just get up, dust myself off a bit, deal with some small amount of dizziness, and continue where I left off. Well, that was wrong because the balance was totally scrambled in my head. I lost the ability to get on my feet and stay on my feet. I knew what my legs should do; I knew what was up, down, left, and right, but without any assistance, I would just collapse on whichever side I leaned to at that moment and probably bust open my head.

I was not expecting that, but everyone else did. That's why nurses were by my side every time I wanted to get out of the bed. They walked with me up and down that room, I placed my hand around nurses' necks, and I slowly but surely started to get better. Once my mother and sister came to visit me, they did the same with me in the hallway, each on one side, and I walked the walk until the final reunion with my balance.

Are You Talking to Me?

How circumstances can change your whole view on the same exact thing, it's incredible. I've witnessed this so many times, and I don't even know why I keep getting surprised.

Earlier in this book, I told you how I got accustomed to specific situations and environments, inevitably, subtly, and against my wishes and plans. That can more often than not end up being a good thing for a person, and the perfect example is the case of me adapting to that initial hospital environment.

Now I was in a new domain, and Father Time got me again. Only one thing needed to happen — I needed to detach from that IV and get off that hospital bed, and before I knew it, that large hospital room became my second home. I had my own place where we sat to eat breakfast, I knew several kids around me, and I managed to get my mind off the recent troubles.

This time, not even the colorful walls were necessary.

But don't think for a second that that environment was a fit replacement for my home. As a matter of fact, given the green light, I would have run out so fast from there that you wouldn't even get the chance to say your goodbyes and best wishes.

Here's proof of that, and this story is something my mother and I discussed and laughed about years later.

It was early, and we'd just had our breakfast. The usual morning routine — you had two slices of bread, and you could choose between honey, jam, or butter. Next to that, you had either milk or tea, which was tea or nothing in my case because I never liked the taste of milk. The food was placed on a small table in our room, next to the wall. I was sitting on the left side, opposite some kid.

Then something unexpected happened — I turned around, and I saw my mom standing by the door. She was smiling, she had a suspiciously happy expression on her face, and the nurse said, "Ivana, you are going home."

I looked at them without saying anything, and because she said the wrong name (like many people did as my mother's name was Ivana), it took me a few seconds to realize they were addressing me.

"Me? I am going home, really?" I replied with a shocked expression on my face and evident excitement in my voice.

"Yes, you!" my mother happily replied.

I couldn't believe my ears, I was absolutely flabbergasted, and because my eyes were wide open, along with my mouth, this became evident to everyone else. I never knew this was coming, and I was not aware that my mom was arriving that day. I certainly had no clue that on this occasion, she was taking me home with her.

This little scene may be uninteresting to somebody else, but that event was something that my mother and I laughed about for quite some time. We giggled as we described the mixture of astonishment and confusion on my face as I received the surprise visit and even more surprising news. I would recreate my facial expression over and over again, and we would burst out laughing.

That's another thing I regret I didn't revisit with her when she was alive. We didn't talk about this for years, and that goes to show you how many times I locked my mind's doors so nobody could get in.

Well, I don't care any more. Late or not, keys or no keys, now I'm busting them open.

The doors I am talking about actually belong to a closet, and it is filled with all kinds of baggage of an untidy, sloppy mind. At this point, the only thing I can do is to let all the crap fall out and just pick up one piece at a time while trying to sort everything out in an orderly manner.

That takes some time, but unless you stop doing it, you will eventually and inevitably get there.

Yellow Brick Road

I had two versions of myself during my early relationship with Zagreb. My post-operation visits were often just a twenty-minute medical consultation with my doctor. This doesn't sound bad, but it was a nightmare for me. Not only did I fear my doctor (even though he was the best and the nicest one you could ever find), but I also knew that he could, and occasionally would, send me on week-long hospital stays. He had the power and control in the most painful area of my life, and I was deathly scared of that.

So in my first version, you have a kid that sleeps all the way to Zagreb because she can't handle the constant thinking about what's coming. That same person will not eat before everything is over because she is sick to her stomach, so offering her food is a waste of time. And when everything gets done, butterflies that raided her belly suddenly disappear, they make room for a sandwich, and you are now traveling home with a kid that is fully awake and doesn't shut up.

This was the usual behavior for me when I was seven and eight, and it didn't change even in my teenage years. An excellent example of this was my trip home after the operation, which I remember quite well. I don't know how my mother managed to drive, to be honest, because I was asking so many questions that I would have, if I had been her, thrown me out of the car.

I was asking about my friends, where they were and what they were doing, and I was really interested to know if somebody had bought a new game for Super Nintendo.

I'd had many trips back and forth before, but this time it was special because the operation was in a rear-view mirror for us, and we were driving pretty fast on that highway.

I may have been only six, but I knew that this was not the final goodbye, or better yet, the final good riddance to the hospital. Despite that, I acted like it was, which was an excellent coping mechanism.

One particular strategy served me well in later years, and the unwritten rule is pretty simple. After you leave Zagreb and you find out the date of your next mandatory visit, spend three-quarters of that time acting as if you will never see that hospital again. In short, if today is January, my return is scheduled for May, I will only start to worry about this as April ends.

Before that, Zagreb does not exist for me.

So this trip home, in my short-term-thinking mind, was my final sayonara to doctors and nurses, and the only things I was concerned with were the girls, boys, and toys that awaited me back home.

Chapter 4: An Action Man Featuring Barbie

I came home for good, so exciting! Like I said earlier, a child's short-term, small-picture way of thinking pays off. I didn't care what position I would be in two, five, or ten years from now. Thinking way ahead was simply not something I would do.

It's like my current friends are the only friends I will ever have. It's like there will never be sobering moments where people around me will go independent, find the love of their life, and eventually start raising a family of their own while I continue with my solitary life. It's not like I've seen the last of the dreadful hospitals and embarrassing examinations.

Some things I just ignored, some of it was impossible for me to predict, so to my young mind, ignorance was bliss.

But while I was looking at that tiny picture, my parents had not only the big picture but also a giant animated billboard in front of them. A billboard that was displaying all my potential life's troubles and putting them in a sleep-sucking loop. My mom didn't seem too worried on the outside, though, but to be fair, for years, she also didn't seem to be sick — yet she was.

If my mother were here now, I would ask her about her mindset during those challenging times.

I assume one of the concerns was my immediate reaction to this new life, even though my behavior before the operation showed no signs of near-future problems. After that, you have the factors that you can't control, and she must've been a little worried about my friends' reactions towards me, which could affect my response to everything else.

Once you leave this tight circle, you have even more fears and dilemmas as school time approaches. This is when parents slowly need to start loosening their grip so they don't lose it involuntarily, and they are forced to leave their vulnerable child on its own in this new environment. All of a sudden, the questions start to build up. Like a rolling snowball — the further you go, the heavier it becomes.

What inquiries will my child have as she grows up? How will my child react to the announced hormonal therapy? What awaits her during complicated teenage years, which are hard enough for normal teenagers? What kind of clothes will she wear? How will she behave? What about dating and sexual preferences? Will she be subjected to prejudice? Will she be able to get a job? What if other medical problems occur? Will she suffer from depression, shyness, or any social disorder?

So on, and so forth. I don't even have to mention the complications that came along with my mother's sickness.

These are some of the questions I, too, would probably have had if I were in my mother's shoes, and it seems pretty complicated and mentally draining. Maybe it would be easier in reality, but I'm sure at least half of these issues weighed heavily on her mind.

If I have to guess, I think she had a strategic approach to this. What I mean is, she decided to pick her battles and set less important issues aside.

There're only so many cans of worms you can afford to open at one time.

A Toy Story

My parents didn't complicate things around the toys I liked to play with, that's for sure. That's why I decided to place "featuring" instead of "versus" into this chapter's name.

You see, when I arrived home, I had many toys, and they contradicted each other if you look at them from the perspective that is imposed on us by society. On the one hand, I had Barbie and Sindy dolls, a Barbie salon, bathroom, and a kitchen, and on the other hand, I had my diver Action Man doll from 1993 (still do, but it's naked), a plastic gas station with moving ramps, a car shop, and a bunch of toys on wheels. Next to that, I had more unisex games, like Super Nintendo.

How to solve this dilemma? I'm sorry, what dilemma? It's easy — just play with everything if that's what you want.

My parents didn't care if I preferred an Action Man with a harpoon, a Sindy doll with angel wings or if I decided to take them both on a diving expedition and to a hairdresser right after that. You think Sindy would never drive to a gas station, and Action Man would never have oily, dry, or split hair? Everything is for everybody at one point or another.

Let's be honest — there's no justified reason to place these kinds of restrictions on your child. The sad thing is, many parents that focus on keeping their child in "the right lane" are failing to instill the values that do matter. Someone hand these people a garbage bag because what they are doing is a waste of time.

Teach your kids that the role of giver makes a receiver out of you. Tell them that if you do something positive for others, you gain it back in a positive manner, too, sometimes even multiplied. Tell your kids that race does not matter, sexual preferences either.

Who cares if your friend is religious and you are not when you can find common ground on so many other life values? Who gives a crap if a family of a person you know comes from a country that was in a war with your homeland many years ago, when peace and love can outweigh and demolish any prejudice with minimum but honest effort? And who cares if you are attracted to people of the same sex, and you wish to get married when nobody, in reality, is threatened because of this?

In a world with ever-growing concerns, challenges and responsibilities, priorities are of the utmost importance. We need to fight the battles that make sense.

Hello, My Friends, Guess What!

I, Ivan, was a very social child. We moved to our current house in the early nineties, when I was about three years old, and I clicked with every single kid in my neighborhood that was approximately my age. We were a very tight group, and every single day out was pure joy.

So I wasn't the only kid that had to get used to my new name. It took a few weeks before my friends got fully used to referring to me as a female. I had lots of friends at the age of six, the same number before and after the surgery. I'm happy to say everybody stuck around, not that I was concerned they wouldn't. In reality, they felt almost no other change except for the name.

So how did they react to a new me? Let me tell you a story about my first encounter with my buddies after I arrived home.

I remember it being very sunny, and it was really beautiful outside. I was inside, and the front door was open so the light would fill in the interior. My mom was sitting on a small kids chair in front of that door, she had a blanket over her legs, and she was enjoying the delightful stream of sunny rays.

The silence was broken when one friend came to my yard. A boy that was three years older than me approached my mom, and he asked her, "Can Ivan come out and play?"

I was still inside, and he was not able to see me, but I heard his question, and I also heard my mom's response to him.

"It's not Ivan any more. Your friend has a new name," she responded and explained the rest in the shortest way possible.

So there it was — the first introduction. I came out, we went to our usual gathering place, my other friends came too, and it was time for me to explain my situation.

How exactly I did that, I don't remember, but what I do recollect is me walking with my one-year-older buddy, who was my closest male friend at the time. Soon after, he got briefed about everything.

"So, how different is it now that you are a girl? What is the difference between being a boy and a girl?" he asked.

"I don't feel any difference — it's the same," I replied while I was walking on the curb on the left side of the road near my house.

That sounds about right in retrospect. I was as honest as I could be. I really didn't feel any difference because no one was forcing me to change. It was just the name — that's all that was different.

At that time, my only job was to eat, sleep, play with my friends, and get used to talking about myself in a female form. I would catch myself making a mistake from time to time, but after three weeks or so, I formed a new habit.

Childhood v.2.0

I had two major groups of friends that lived close to each other but never really interacted with each other in everyday life. But I was close to both of these squads. One was a male group, which was filled with boys of my age or older, and the other was a female group, which was a bit smaller in number and overall younger than me.

While my female friends were too young to comprehend my situation, my male buddies were more than willing to discuss this, up until one point when it wasn't an exciting topic any more.

In the end, nothing was different. Every male game there was, I played it, and I liked it, and there was no scalpel in this world that would be able to change that.

Are we playing war? Cool! How about soccer? Even better! We were outside all the time — before school, after school, on weekends, regularly. We were truly as free as a child can be. We were little risk-takers; sometimes we did things we weren't supposed to, like climbing into houses that were in the early stages of construction and packed with sharp nails. We didn't care about the boards, nails, spider webs, and mud, and we didn't concern ourselves with cars as roads in our block were pretty much vehicle-free most of the time.

Our parents trusted us, and we showed our appreciation for that trust by respecting our limits and staying safe and alive.

Thinking about this makes me realize how location affects the way you are brought up.

If you live in an area with heavy traffic, or if you have the misfortune of raising your kid in a bad neighborhood, of course, there is a higher chance you will be more protective of your child. Helicopter parenting is not precisely the ideal way of raising a child, and I think we can all agree that less freedom means the kid is missing out on some crucial early life experiences.

That's why I consider myself lucky, because nothing dangerous was lurking where my friends and I lived.

The Pain Behind Closed Doors

My friends knew a lot about me, but they knew little about my adversities. They had no idea about the exact reasons for my occasional trips to Zagreb after the operation, and they were unaware of the emotional and physical pain I faced during every trip.

The reason was simple: I forgot all about my troubles the second I left that doctor's office, and I refused to relive them. My fun-time was much too valuable.

And to be perfectly honest, nothing I had to say about it would be of interest to a bunch of pre-teen kids.

I was not about to talk about vaginal dilation routines, by far the most painful experiences in my life. I would rather shoot myself in the shoulder than relive any of those "therapies" all over again, and I had to go through that many times.

My friends never knew how every single trip was precisely the same. Never easier, and it made me sick every time.

First, I lost my appetite a week before that Monday trip. Second, my stomach was tied in knots, and it got worse as we approached Zagreb. After we arrived, we waited in line for my name to be called so we could visit the surgeon. He never did anything on the spot, he would just send us to the very floor I lived in after the operation, and my mom and I would sit in a waiting room. An hour or two would pass, and he would appear, which would make my heart sink to darkness-filled depths.

It never got better, it never got easier, and the reason was the extreme discomfort and pain I felt during that "routine." I couldn't take it, I was frozen with fear, and the surgeon was not helping at all. Moreover, he seemed to get annoyed by my expressions of pain, as he repeated over and over again that it hurt only because I didn't relax my body.

"Keep your butt down, Ivana, keep your butt down," he said every single time, and not once did he call me by my actual name.

"Oh, come on, it doesn't hurt much," he said, trying to assure me just as often.

Just when I thought I couldn't feel any shittier, he decided to compare me to some other patient.

"The girl that was here fifteen minutes before you, how come she felt no pain? Come on, it does not hurt that much."

Well, it does, thank you very much.

One of these visits is the reason I cried in front of my mom. If you remember, I mentioned this previously.

As a result of all of this, I once approached the nurse who was in charge of handing the instruments, and I asked her if we could do all of this under anesthesia. She said no, so we continued with the "torture".

However, because of my question, my next appointment was a four-day hospital stay, and they did the same under general anesthesia. I later saw in my papers which size of the instruments they were using, and I realized how far he could afford to go when I couldn't express any pain. He would always gradually increase the size, and with it the amount of pain, but in this case, I was removed from the equasion. My ass was down and out.

I was sick of seeing their faces. I was tired of going through this torture, and I was also tired of the burning sensation I felt while peeing during every first visit to the bathroom after this procedure.

If I ever felt like my life-saving operation was a waste of time, this was it. In my mind, nothing was worth this trouble because I felt like the worst was, after all, not over, and shit kept piling up. It never seemed like I could see the end of it, and it was all confirmed when I was told I would have to do this on a regular basis, especially "when you find a boyfriend."

This is something that a gynecologist told me, some lady that had never seen me before in my life. It angered me because by listening to her, you could quickly realize that she had a very shallow insight into my medical history. She was under the impression that my main objective was to find a boyfriend like I was the one that asked for this life. At least do your basic research.

In reality, the truth couldn't be more different. Mom tried her best to ease me into this life, and she did everything in her power to make this transition as painless as possible. But I didn't walk my way into this story — I was parachuted in.

So my friends knew nothing about this. Only my mother and I realized what a seemingly simple trip to some other town really meant.

Chapter 5: Self-Consciousness and Shame

Kids are curious by nature and extremely eager to feed that curiosity. On top of that, you can bet that surprising information, especially a juicy subject like mine, will spread very quickly.

Another thing kids are, is open, sometimes without a filter. When you combine that with an undeveloped sense for awkward situations and other people's psychological suffering, you get what I got as a teenager.

In my life, there were many small but uncomfortable encounters with kids I wish I could erase from my memory. Many of the memories did fade, but some hurt me too much at that moment for me to forget. To be clear, I never got physically hurt by anyone because of this, and I was never the subject of repetitive verbal abuse.

Instances I'm about to describe to you all have the same theme, and every single account was short but had a long-lasting resonance in my head. None of them seem bad on the face of it, I'll admit it, but I had to include them in this list because they did affect me the most.

Why? Well, I'll do my best to explain.

Are You a Boy or a Girl?

What a boring question. I say boring because I heard it so often. It was so repetitive that I developed a sense for it. I could smell it a mile away, let alone across the hallways, where it was brought up the most.

I had to look a kid in the eyes only once to figure out what was coming. So this one time, I looked at the boy across this empty hallway, and my spidey sense went off immediately. A few seconds after that, he asked a question that would make me rich if it came along with a nickel.

"Are you a boy or a girl?" he said.

My heart sank, and my stomach twisted into a knot like it did every time someone decided to satisfy their curiosity in this manner.

The difference is, this time I decided to answer the question instead of ignoring it and walking away.

I said to this boy, "I'm a girl." I felt satisfied that I finally decided to stand up for myself in a way. I thought that this would make him go away, but I was wrong. He did not ask that because he wanted to know. He asked because he had his responses ready, and he just needed me to set him up for a punchline.

"A girl? Yeah right…" he replied instantly with a smirk on his face. He got what he wanted.

He didn't believe me, and that was a punch to the gut. It was a very tough thing to swallow because he said the exact same thing I wanted to avoid by not responding. The truth really hurts the most — I know that for a fact.

In reality and all honesty, I really could have been mistaken for a boy in several parts of my life when I had shorter hair. But these kinds of passive attacks were more often than not planned because these kids had plenty of other ways to inform themselves if they were so interested in knowing this one fact about me.

The thing is, they did inform themselves, and then they proceeded with the question just to have some fun. I can remember them staring at my eyes, and I can just see the wheels turning in their heads.

She was a boy; now she's a girl. How is this possible? What is this?

I was Bigfoot to them.

The pieces of my story were sometimes too intriguing because here I was, looking sort of like a girl, dressing like a boy and acting like something in-between.

I really can't blame anyone, but I can't blame myself either. Those kids were not the only ones confused; I was puzzled, too. I didn't know how to act outside my home turf bubble. I didn't know how to dress, and the only thing I knew was that I would not wear anything too girly. There was no way.

This incident resulted in a much greater sense of shame. The reason was my age; I was older here, about thirteen. What's more important, the kid that hurt me was the same age as me, maybe even a year older, so there's less excuse to be found for his behavior.

There were no two ways about it, he was being straight-up mean, and his only goal was to shame me and to make his friends laugh at the same time.

This happened in one of my childhood friend's houses, away from my comfort zone. The problem here was the location. She lived outside my town, and I knew nothing about the group of friends she was surrounded with at the time of my arrival. I knew her very well, but her friends were complete strangers to me. This was actually the first time I was seeing most of them.

My mother and I arrived; we entered the house. She sat down in their dining room with my friend's mom, and this time I sat down with them.

The reason for that was the realization that there were a bunch of other kids behind closed bedroom doors. I could hear them, but I couldn't see them. I was not interested in knowing exactly who was there because I knew I should not mingle with anybody on that particular visit. My spidey sense advised strongly against it.

I had every intention of listening to my gut feeling, but unfortunately, the pressure from my friend's mother was too much. She kept telling me to join their play, and I eventually went, against my better judgment.

I entered the room; I closed the door behind me. They were staring at me, and right there I realized I was in my worst nightmare. They were playing Truth or Dare — the last game I wanted to participate in.

I stood there; I was only watching, not playing.

"Play with us," someone from that group asked me.

"Nah, I'm just gonna watch," I replied.

I don't know who kept insisting I should play, but I eventually gave in, and soon it was going to be my turn to face the truth or dare.

Participation was rotating in a clockwise motion, and my turn arrived. I was already a bit overweight, weirdly dressed, and I was feeling ugly, so being stared at by unfamiliar kids did not actually make me feel comfortable. To be more precise, it made me want to jump out of my skin.

"Truth or dare?" I was asked by the boy.

I weighed the options in my head even before I started to play, and since I was not in the mood to embarrass myself by doing something physical, I decided in advance that I would pick truth.

You see, I was naïve for a second. I actually hoped that, in the end, I would not be tossed into the lion's cage on my first turn.

I was, of course, wrong, and my spidey sense was right.

"Are you a boy or a girl?"

The question was fired out immediately.

I couldn't believe that this kind of shit was still happening to me.

I only knew how to run, so I decided to leave the room moments after my friend intervened by explaining to others that this was a silly question.

Unfortunately, this event turned out to be pretty pricey because after that I stopped visiting my friend altogether. We were there almost weekly, and this lasted for years, but just like that, her house ended up being one more location on my "to avoid" list.

There was simply no way I was gonna allow myself to fall into the same trap once again.

Locker-Room Talk

I was ten years old this time, and this situation escalated in a girls' locker room before handball practice.

The training was about to start, I was already dressed to play and ready for action, but for some reason, I had to go back to our locker room, where several other girls were. One was my classmate; the other one did not know me at all. So I went there, and all of a sudden, the kid I didn't know got startled when she saw me entering the locker room.

"Oh my god, for a second I thought that a boy entered," she yelled out as she continued to get dressed.

This is where my classmate decided to tell her she was not that far off.

"Well, Ina was actually a boy before. Right, Ina?"

I just stood there for a few seconds, silent, not knowing what to do. You can already guess what I did then — I walked away.

All these stories have something in common — I had short hair in all of them. And another common thing is my reaction. There was never a "fight or flight" option for me. Flight was the only way I knew how to deal with such adversity.

This incident didn't hurt as much as the other two I mentioned, but it got stuck in my head — and I think I know why. This was the first time a girl made me uncomfortable. Before that, mostly boys had something to say out loud and to my face.

The other reason for remembering this so vividly was the unknown aftermath. You see, if there was a single, less-known person involved, like in the first case, I would have shrugged it off more easily because I didn't care as much about what that person did with that information. But if there were two or more kids, and at least one of them was somebody I knew, I was not able to let it go that easily. That's because after leaving, I continued to think about the kids involved and how they were probably still talking about me after I left.

That rewinding of the tape, I assume, caused the story to be burned into my brain.

This fourth story involved the largest group of people, but it was the least traumatic, probably because I was fifteen or sixteen at the time, and the main goal of the person that approached me was to make me feel better.

I was sitting at my desk, the class was about to end, and I felt a tap on my shoulder. I turned around, and I was given a note from a friend sitting in the back of the row. I unfolded the piece of paper, and then blood suddenly rushed to my face while my heart started to beat twice as fast.

This was, more or less, what the note said:

—I heard what happened to you. I want you to know that we support you—

I folded the paper back, and I went quiet. But after the class was over, she sat next to me; she asked me if I saw the note. I nodded yes, and I replied nothing else; I couldn't even look her in the eyes.

This sounds like it turned out quite nice, and she truly had the best intentions, but back then, it was a problem.

Number one, I suddenly realized that I was the topic of conversation in the entire classroom, and I knew it would remain that way for some period of time. And number two, when she said "they" support me, I knew she couldn't be talking on behalf of everyone, so I was still worried about what would happen in the next few days as this thing spread even more. Also, I was worried about misinformation.

In reality, nothing happened. Nobody asked me about it, nobody was that interested in the details, and you guessed it — that suited me just fine.

Actually, I had a sense of peace at least because the cat was out of the bag.

The Psychiatrist's Office

Kids weren't the only ones that could make me feel anxious and ashamed. I felt uncomfortable around professionals other than my doctor, too.

I don't know how tough a psychiatrist's job is, but I'm sure it's a very challenging occupation. It's tough enough to deal with a stationary problem, where there is one clear instruction manual for fixing it. But when you deal with human beings, you are starting over every time a new person enters the office. A new client, a new set of problems, and a unique, yet-to-be-discovered pathway to a potential solution.

I have only one real experience with a physician in this branch of medicine that I can remember, and I can't say it was a good one. Despite that, I'm aware of the importance of diagnosis, study, and treatment of mental disorders. I also recognize that one session is too small of a sample, so I'm not exactly in a position to judge.

Who knows, maybe I even made some progress during that first and only experience. If you're a professional, you can perhaps let me know.

I was about fourteen when I was called to the office to have an open talk. I entered the room and immediately felt uneasy. It was not a sight from the movies: no comfortable chairs, no sense of privacy. Instead of that, I faced a young person that was obviously testing out her newly acquired skills on me.

To add to the weirdness, there was a young doctor behind me that was writing something on a PC. It seemed like he was doing something unrelated, so I was wondering why he was there in the first place.

She started asking me questions, simple ones, and her intentions were evident from the start. Her tactic was transparent — she was buttering me up and trying to make a smooth transition to hot questions.

What's my name, how old I am, where do I live, what school do I go to… nothing complicated.

Then the real questions came. I knew it — she was trying to get me to tell my own story out loud.

"Tell me more about your condition?" she said.

"Everything is available in my medical files," I replied as a true smartass.

But she insisted.

"What happened to you at the age of six," she asked.

"I had surgery," I responded.

"What kind of surgery was it?" she asked

"My files have all the information," smartass in me insisted.

But she wouldn't let it go, and in the end, I told her I had sex change surgery.

Then she asked the final question. "Do you feel like a girl?"

There was a moment of silence, but I answered yes to get her off my back.

This was when the session ended, and I left the room.

What happened next was very typical for me. I entered the nearest bathroom, and I cried.

Was this a breakthrough? I can't say it was because nothing changed for me outside the hospital. As you can see, it took me a long time to open up.

Chapter 6: Self-Destruction

All the problems, trials, and tribulations I faced, I would gladly multiply by a thousand and suffer through everything if that would have spared my mother the illness that started in 1995 and ended in 2016 when she passed away.

It was 1995. The very first day of my first grade was the very first day of her dialysis. What started as a black dot in her field of vision was ultimately diagnosed as kidney failure, and her life suddenly became dependent on machines.

For people who are not familiar with this, the machine, called a dialyzer, filters a person's blood outside the body and circles it back. That remained the only way to get rid of the metabolic toxins and excess water, which is what kidneys usually do. My mom lived this way for twenty years.

Even though dialysis is a miracle of medicine, the body still suffers, it ages quickly, and all of this takes a toll on a person's mental health, as well.

My visits to the specialist happened on Mondays from that day on because my mom was on dialysis every Tuesday, Thursday, and Saturday. This meant that if I had to go to Zagreb, her Tuesdays were extra hard, especially in an earlier period where she traveled to the same city for this treatment.

My mom died in 2016. She collapsed and did not survive despite my attempt at CPR. It was terrible, horrifying, and it was everything I ever feared. I did a bad job with the CPR, and it took me about six months to stop rewinding every single moment of the event. I was trying to remember every detail in a desperate attempt to alleviate the guilt, but at the same time, I was afraid of the opposite scenario, where I would remember some new way I could have assisted, but hadn't.

I have never convinced myself I did everything in my power because I know I did a poor job. But after a year, I just learned to live with that.

I didn't know what to do, and I felt fake. People were sending me their condolences, and I thanked every single one of them with a soft, gentle tone of voice. At the same time, I was thinking to myself that my mom could still be alive if I had handled the situation better, and I hated myself for trying to justify my sorry-ass attempt while explaining to everyone else what in the world had happened to my mother.

They all knew she was very sick, but almost none of them knew much about her real condition or what dialysis meant in general. As my mom got sicker, she spent less and less time with other people. So many were unaware of the circumstances. Because of that, they were justifiably shocked when she passed away.

Terrible Silver Lining

The circumstances around my mom's death are not the only thing that spawned guilt in my head. The other source of this feeling was actually a positive thing — my move to Zagreb.

During my most challenging times, I was dreading big moves, so much so that a series of bad events had to happen for me to snap out of it and leave my zone. The first significant thing was a car crash.

Six months before my mom died, she and I drove to a town fifty kilometers away. She was driving as I didn't have a driver's license back then, and we arrived safely at our destination. But on our way home, my mom became so exhausted as a result of the examination, she blacked out halfway back, in the middle of our ride.

Without braking, while I was looking at my phone, we flew off the road and right into the woods in a straight line. We ended up on our side, the wheels were trashed and unable to turn, the car engine fell out, and the car doors became sealed shut.

I screamed, "Mom!"

She opened her eyes, and then she said, "F*ck, I fell asleep."

Right then, I jumped out the car's window, and with the help of a person that saw the whole thing, I flipped the car back on its now useless wheels so my mom could exit the crumpled can.

I didn't even have a scratch on me, and she had just one. But when the guy saw her hand, he thought that she had broken her bone in several places. In reality, he was looking at the lumps and bumps where the needle from the dialyzer went in.

This event pushed me to get a loan from a bank, buy a car, and pay for my driver's license. At the same time, I started a graphic design course, and I was now able to drive myself to it a few times a week.

I was driving on the very road we almost lost our lives on.

We did survive, that was one more thing we did together, but in January 2016, our story ended. Once again, I was there with her, but this time I managed to do absolutely nothing.

After my mom passed away, I struggled a lot with staying at home, and in the end, I did something I never thought I would do — I moved to Zagreb.

All my dark predictions and fears never materialized. Quite the opposite, I've learned a lot by living where my job is. I made amazing new friends, and I became independent.

The problem is, I don't know if I would have ever done that if my mother were alive today, and that has been bothering me ever since I got some guts and faced my fears. I assumed I would stay in "avoidance mode," which could make it look like she was somehow responsible for my failure to progress in life, and that's not true. But I feel incredibly guilty for this hypothetical scenario, and while it has faded with time, I still can't shake it off completely.

I want to make this very clear — she never cuffed me or guilt-tripped me. She would be the happiest person in the world if I were to make it on my own. She most certainly believed I could do it because she kept telling me I was smart and capable. So while I'm glad I'm in Zagreb, I'm mad at myself for ever intertwining my mom with my excuses.

One example of this was a job offer from my old boss, which would have required me to move to Serbia. I refused to go, and in my mind, I was thinking about how I didn't want to miss out on any time with my mom, as it was pretty limited. But I was a coward and nothing more. Excuses, excuses.

I learned a lot from this, and now I know that a list of possible problems, which could be endless if you look hard enough, should sometimes be put aside.

We'll Manage It

If you need more proof of how self-destructive I was, I've got plenty of examples to share. Don't do this at home, kids.

I never had food or drug allergies, but I was allergic to some words. One of the phrases I was hypersensitive to was said by Mother on many occasions.

"We'll manage it," she would say while we were debating whether we could afford something or not. The moment she said that, I gave up on whatever small thing we were trying to buy. I didn't want us to struggle financially because of something we could live without.

As a result of my reactions, she eventually restrained herself from using this phrase around me.

But now I understand the benefits of its occasional usage. Sometimes you just have to take a risk and believe your gut instinct that everything will turn out OK in the end.

That turned out to be one of the forces that twisted that corkscrew, and everything I bottled up slowly started to be released. I have learned that it's not only fine to take more significant risks at times, but it's mandatory.

A Screw-up

When I try to compare my present self with my teenage version, I find lots of differences, drastic ones. I wish I knew then what I know now because I would probably make different decisions after eighth grade.

I chose a three-year trade school because it was available in my hometown, but I had way more potential than that. I simply did not want to leave home, that was never an option for me, and I did myself a huge disservice.

My mom told me that it was my decision, and she pointed out to me that she did not want me ever to blame her if I ended up regretting it.

I did regret it, but I only have myself to blame.

When I think about it from different perspectives, my absence would have meant that I would have spent five, six, or more years less with my mother than I did. So should I feel regret when I think about it like that? Not really, because every moment spent with my mother was precious to me.

But I do recognize now that the less convenient option would have been more beneficial for all parties. Again, everything circles back to making excuses.

In the end, against the odds, my stories have a positive outcome. Luckily, I don't work in the particular occupation that I went to school for, and the people that I met in Zagreb helped re-spark my desire to live.

As The World Turns

I was such a promising child; I had such a beautiful childhood, but nothing lasts forever — we all know that. The difference with me was when one door closed, the other one failed to open all the way. I was not truly ready for anything monumental in my life, so I peeked out just to see what was out there. Then I quickly ran back in. Sissy.

While my friends spent their late teenage years thinking about the future and education they would pick as they moved away from their homes, I was slowly closing the door of my room, where the PC was.

That PC came just in time to become a distraction from the reality of my existence. I squandered parts of my life with it, while I also gained weight and lost the little self-confidence I had.

I still hung out with some of my friends, but those activities, which were once precious to me, became too rare.

My buddies had their friends from school, that circle became bigger and bigger, and I simply considered myself too weird, too pathetic, too ugly, too short, and too unworthy for any of it. I lacked an identity, I was embarrassed, the social gatherings started to drain my energy, I was unhappy, and all I ever wanted was to go home.

Members of my family occasionally tried to explain to me what I needed to change in my life, but I never wanted to listen. I rejected every criticism, and I would get mad. I was stubborn, I wore baggy clothes because I felt like it, and if anyone tried to comment on anything, my feelings would, again, get hurt.

Also, I was on hormone replacement therapy from the age of fourteen, and that started right after the medication that was supposed to "simulate" a menstrual cycle every month. Fortunately, the pill situation didn't go with the flow, as a period was the last thing I needed. I was happy because of that, but on the other hand, this was one more thing I could not discuss with others because I didn't have it.

So bye-bye, my friends, and good luck on your journey. I'm just going to stay here and suffocate in my own bubble.

Suddenly, the comfort zone became toxic to me. It's like starting a car engine in a large but closed-up area. Eventually, the gasses were reaching near-lethal levels, and I knew I had to get out.

So, in the end, me and me friends did similar things in life, but the difference is, I had to destroy myself to re-build myself because my old version was not working any more. This took years, and that's why I arrived late.

But better late than never.

Chapter 7: Rock Bottom

People around me know I never misused the cards life dealt me. Not only that, but I'm also pretty sure I did myself some fair amount of disservice by underrating everything about myself, my abilities, and the misfortunes I had in life.

Nevertheless, I can be clear-headed instead of pig-headed about that, at least for a second while writing this book, and pat myself on the back while saying, "You did go through a lot."

I did deal with all sorts of emotions, like waves of depression, ever since my teenage years, yet I never physically came close to doing anything to myself. I realized a long time ago that I don't have the courage to do that, which was an interesting realization.

Why? Well, so many people like to label the poor souls who commit suicide as cowards. But how can someone do something others are afraid to do and be a coward at the same time?

So, with me feeling the way I felt at times, and it could have been anywhere between slightly bad to pretty shitty, there was never a situation where I was one step away from kissing a train or swallowing a fistful of pills.

Even so, I must say I sometimes feel a bit nervous about that in general. There are so many unexpected deaths of this kind in the world that it makes it look like any human being can have a short circuit in the brain and do the unimaginable. The fact is, people take their own lives all the time, and I cannot imagine the pain they must feel at that moment.

I thought my pain was bad enough, yet their suffering must be a thousand times worse. These are the depths I don't ever want to explore. Unfortunately, that deadly deed can also be impulsive and poorly thought through. Nevertheless, it's just as final.

When you compare a depressed but stable person to a suicidal person, it's clear that psychological pain is something they both have in common. The difference is, a depressed but stable person wants to alleviate pain, and a suicidal person wants to end it. We all know that life can never be painless, and whoever wants to finish their life's path sees no reason to put up with any amount of hurt. At least that's the way I understand it.

I assume most people would agree on what the telltale signs for suicide look like, but I don't think many can easily recognize them unless they come in a bundle.

If we only see an increase in risky behavior, it's not as apparent as it would be if someone started giving away his or her prized possessions and continued to talk about death. If someone "only" decreases his social activity, it doesn't look as alarming as it would be if that person started talking about suicide and casually said a final goodbye to their family and friends.

In reality, there are many potential red flags, like mood swings, anxiety, increased consumption of drugs, panic attacks, isolation, expressions of regret, talk about being a burden to other people, et cetera. How much will end up being too much for someone varies from person to person.

If you recognize these signs in yourself or someone else and you see a worrisome pattern, please react or just contact your local suicide prevention helpline.

Nihilistic Thoughts

Did I look at myself as a third wheel and a person with absolutely no meaning and value in the world? Yes, at times.

I will never have my own biological kids, so I felt I could not contribute to society in that way, too. But hey, even an appendix, once considered completely useless, turned out to be a useful organ and home to all kinds of good bacteria.

There must be something worthwhile about my existence; there must be. I kept repeating that in my head.

I don't want to spread any negative energy, but I would like to share with you one situation where my thinking turned bad. These were potentially my saddest thoughts, and they occurred about a year and a half after my mother passed away.

I sat down at my computer desk, I stared at the screen for a few minutes, and then I decided to open up a blank text document. At that time, I was a part-time journalist, next to my normal job, but this time I wasn't going to write anything mixed martial arts-related.

Instead of that, I decided to type down the names of people who were close to me, and I gave all of them a certain number. The numerical value, from one to ten, represented the level of sadness the individual would be struck with if I suddenly died. Number one meant that the person would not give two shits about my permanent absence, and number ten represented an unbearable amount of sadness.

So I wrote out the list, which turned out to be depressingly small, and I typed out the values. Most of the names received values lower than five, a few had six to nine, and I think only two or three people had a ten.

Then I decided to add it all up, divide it by the number of participants, and that way, I would have the average digit. After I did that, the final number was five, and five would mean you would feel some sense of loss, but after three or four weeks, you would already be able to live your life without dwelling on the fact that I am gone.

Boy, my self-pity, unlike me, was going places. And you know what, that average number seemed about right. I was typing those digits out with whole honesty.

I stared at them; I felt uneasy by the realization, but I saw it as the truth — and we all know that the truth hurts at times.

At that point, my sorrow told me what I should do. For the first time in a long time, my thoughts sobered me up, and things became clearer than ever. It took some figuring out after that, but I finally knew my next move. I needed to get out there, I needed to collect more of those numbers, I needed a greater sample, and in the end, I needed a better average value.

That's what everybody should strive for. If you want to be valued and, in the end, missed, come out of that shell and expose yourself so people outside your family don't forget about you.

Recognize and React

It's a horrible thing to get lost and lose control. It's tough to feel like life is a dull, painful, endless cycle or a tape that rolls and rewinds over and over again until everything finally falls apart.

The feelings of this matter should certainly not be ignored, and if some of you do feel this way, the issue should be seriously reviewed and looked at and preferably shared with some other individual or a group of people.

I know sometimes it seems like silence and isolation are the most comforting and soothing options during our rough periods, but I strongly advise people to share their troubles with their loved ones. Or just pick up a phone and call them to hear their voice, to talk to them about anything.

That's the beauty of talking to friends — those conversations need no particular subject to be interesting, beneficial, relaxing, and enjoyable. You just feel good after these interactions, and not even a silence is awkward.

To me, it always came down to breaking that ice. It was apparent to me that it got built up too quickly, and I was getting tired of smashing through it over and over again. My energy got drained even thinking about it, so more often than not, I picked avoidance.

A good example of this is hanging out with people, and I'm sure many people have had this experience. You get nervous before you see a person, for various reasons; you eventually see that person, and you realize that the anxiety was unjustified. Then you feel that if you met them tomorrow, everything would be a lot easier.

But you don't see that friend the next day — you see your friend in two or three weeks — and by that time you realize that the ice is right back where it once was. As a result of that, the next encounter is just as nerve-wracking.

Does that sound familiar?

You Only Get One Shot

The life that we live in is truly unparalleled, and it's unfortunate that someday, it has to end. I guess that's the reason it's so special and precious — at one point, every person will cease to exist.

I think about the long road of human history, and I can't help but ask how come I am alive and alert now, at this exact moment. Why now, and not a hundred, two hundred or three hundred years ago, or one hundred years from now? Could it be that we are always conscious, but as someone else?

The lack of consciousness is so out of reach of comprehension to me that every time I think about it, it leaves me more confused than before.

I've been under anesthesia a few times in my life, and I've sensed its deepness. Normal sleep is nothing in comparison. It's not nearly as relaxing. When I was under, I might as well have been in outer space, and I did wonder many times, *Is this what death feels like?*

When my thoughts were in their darkest form, I reached one of the turning points in the flow of my nihilistic way of thinking. I've come to one crucial and obvious realization — if I truly am at the point where death looks like a better option than life, then what am I worrying about? My supposed wish will inevitably come true, as death is something that awaits us all.

In that case, there is no need to rush anything because years fly too fast anyway. And if nothing is rushed, then there's a chance new values and goals will be discovered, and that person will be glad nothing ended prematurely.

I thought to myself, *If I prefer life over death, and I see its fundamental values, then this relatively short time on Earth should actually be lived out.*

I don't know if we will ever unlock or unveil the mysteries that puzzle not just me but most people, but I would just like to mention that I feel privileged to be living in these times. If there's only one single tape of consciousness for each of us, I can say that I am glad mine is being played right now, alongside yours.

Play it right so that one day, when we are old, every single one of us will have a greatest hits compilation worthy of revisiting.

Survival

Like I said before, my childhood was second to none. As I also mentioned earlier in this book, on the other hand, my adult life was dog shit at times. The battlefield I was on had fewer allies on it because I gradually pushed people away, and I felt exposed, susceptible to being hurt, and alone.

Inevitably, I reached the point of "do or die," so I concluded that if I don't do most of the work in this whole idea of reviving myself, then I don't deserve to be helped by others. Who am I, and how silly would it be for me to expect sympathy and help if I don't feel like helping myself? In my eyes, it would be unfair to give others a piece of the burden that I'm not willing to carry on my own.

Now, I'm not saying my line of thinking was a hundred percent logical or healthy — I'm just transcribing my thoughts.

So I had work to do, and I was forced to improvise.

I call my ways of getting by "improvisation" because I based everything on gut feeling, without talking to others or reading any potentially helpful and insightful literature. I would just say to myself that I should do something about my current state, as a cold sweat would overwhelm me, and more often than not, I would do it.

One thing I did — I got physical. My fears were so in-your-face aggressive that I had to fight back. So I combined physical activity — either I was on an elliptical machine, which I managed to break three times in a one-year period, or I was hitting the bags in my homemade gym in the attic. On occasion, I was running, and every day I was walking my dogs, sometimes for two or three hours. Since I basically had no social life by that point, working out became everything, and the feeling it gave me became an addiction.

Now I'm not nearly as active as I was before, but I still walk to work when I can, or I ride a bike on the same route, which is a two-hour round trip, and I love rollerblading, too. Headphones on my head, wind in my hair, and challenging my blood to do a faster lap through my body — all of this played a life-saving role.

One thing I noticed is I was starting my workouts tired, and I was finishing them pumped up. Because of that, it immediately became obvious that previous exhaustion was not physical — it was psychological.

There is one other method I use. I try to make sure something is always happening in my life because I do feel like I can slip at any moment. To be honest, I feel like a recovered alcoholic who was in so deep that one drop of alcohol would undo every single effort to get sobered up. I feel like it's too risky to relax, and I see keeping a constant focus as a necessity.

So the battle continues, and I like the activity for the most part. It's refreshing to me despite the fact I have an introverted personality. I am very self-aware, I can be quiet around people, I have a tiny group of close friends, and social gatherings outside my closest group can quickly drain my energy. But what keeps me optimistic is the fact that I am better than before, so progress can be, and was, made. I don't know what the limits are, but my goal is to find out.

As this journey continues, doubtful thoughts occasionally arrive and enter my head uninvited. What if all of this is simply putting some lipstick on my ugly troubles? What if I am only doing a superficial job, making my problems look prettier than they actually are, and real demons still hide underneath and are ready to jump on me at any second once they are finished quietly feeding on my suppressed feelings?

I guess that's something I will find out, too. But I am writing these pages, and you are reading them, so maybe my reinvention isn't just a mere illusion and a cheap trick.

Chapter 8: Boys Will Be Boys

I've voluntarily run plenty of scenarios in my head from time to time. That's before I realized that overthinking about certain things can tire me and give me headaches.

Maybe one particular question that took most of my energy never had any purpose since I was placing myself in unrealistic scenarios, but this time I had no control over it. These ponderings just randomly popped into my brain, and I was forced to overintellectualize.

The question I asked myself sounds like this: Would I make the same decision for myself if I were in my parents' shoes?

Let's talk about that some more.

A Thought Experiment

Imagine me going back in time, armed with all the information I placed in this book and all the emotions that cannot be explained with a pen and telling my parents what to do.

In this thought experiment, I am looking at Ivan, I am weighing all the options, and I am trying to figure out if the benefits really have more weight than the cost that awaits him.

When I think about my decision in this fictional time travel episode, it's tough for me to ignore all the negative aspects of the resolution that was made in the early '90s. I'm familiar with the pain of the procedures and psychological agony I've suffered through, and I would have to take a step back and ask myself, *Was it worth it?*

The easiest thing in the world would be to simply conclude, *Well, I am alive*, but it's not as straightforward as that.

Interestingly enough, if I had to decide on behalf of some other kid's parents, I would tell them to go through with everything that was advised by the experts, and I would have zero doubt in my head about what I said. But I would have to think long and hard about little Ivan's situation, and I would try one more time to find some alternate, easier path for that little boy to take.

In the end, I guess I would have no choice but to give up and simply mimic what my mom and dad did, as no safer alternatives were available at that time.

Because of this, if I could visit my younger self in the past or some alternate dimension, I would rather have the advisory role for my teenage self because, in this period, I struggled the most.

I would tell myself that criticism from people should be subject to serious review and consideration and should not be mistaken for an attack. Also, one more piece of crucial advice would include my activity levels and eating habits, which took a turn for the worst in those days. Along with that, I would pull the plug on that damn computer for twenty-two hours a day.

In the end, I can't find fault in my parents' way of thinking in those decision-making moments. There's not much you can do with tied hands.

Mind's Contradiction

I noticed something interesting while playing this game in my mind — it seems like I'm harsh and ruthless towards myself.

Compassionate and kind — those are the words some people use to describe my approach to other human beings. But it seems to me like my attitude is cold as ice when my own fate is at stake.

I'm not sure if this is what self-critical people usually do, and I don't know if this is just a product of a person's desire to become more resilient and tougher. All I know is that I would not treat other people this way.

This is what confuses me. On one side, you have a very defensive person with her shield always on, that will not let you criticize her, touch her, or hurt her in any way, shape, or form. On the other hand, you have a kid that does not hold herself in high regard. That person would say to herself that she is stupid, ugly, unworthy of anything and that the world would not miss much if she was gone.

This is where question marks appear over my head because all of these lines of thinking were mine — at the same time. So I also asked myself, *If I shield myself from even the most benign threats, which would indicate that I care about myself, why do I, at the same time, hate my own reflection and everything I stand for?*

What is it, did I like the person I was and the person I was becoming, or not?

I probably liked my good sides, and I hated the side that stopped me from progressing in life. For example, I probably liked that I'm a good person, but I hated my anxiety, which stopped me from connecting to more people.

That kind of makes sense.

B-Side

From the stories I've heard, my dad was a mischievous kid. He was good and well-intentioned, but he had a habit of causing some amount of trouble, you know, typical of a young male child. But since this was in the '50s and early '60s, we are talking about some light hen-house damage, stealing eggs, and chasing chickens.

I always felt like I was a bit like him before the age of seven. Shyness was practically non-existent, and I was so bold and brash that you would think I had three balls instead of two malfunctioning ones. Actually, my theory is that the surgery stopped me from becoming a pretty troublesome teenager, the kind of boy that would low-key love his parents but who would make them reevaluate their child-raising methods from time to time.

Maybe I'm completely wrong on this one, and the kindness that people point out I now possess is something I would channel out to this degree even if I never faced this fate. But I am very much convinced that everything that happened to me did kick me down a few notches. Not only the operation itself but also the shame that manifested and accumulated as I entered the real world, which was populated by the curious kids I didn't know.

I see this in the way people who managed to stick with me reflect on our friendship. On more than a few occasions, a friend would tell me how he or she had been completely wrong about me. What was a quiet individual who holds back and looks stoned and afraid is actually a moderately intelligent person who can act silly and say some random, weird, and sometimes even funny shit.

The writing of this book actually became one more stitch in this tapestry because just when my more recent friends thought that they knew me fairly well, I dropped a bombshell on them by sending everyone the "Introduction" part of this book.

The difference now is, I am still the same person to them. They've known me long enough. There's just a new layer to me and no more secrets.

This was one more reason for the creation of this book. We all know what even a single secret can do to a friendship.

Learned Behavior

Sometimes I feel manufactured. I hear myself talk, I see myself act, and I think to myself, *These small feminine traits are not real — they are acted out.*

They are learned behavior. I'm not sure how to act differently and, to be honest, I don't feel the need to do that. I have some small traces of guy traits, nothing exaggerated, and I am perfectly fine with keeping them.

What would I be like minus all my troubles? Your guess is as good as mine, but it was fun to think about it from time to time.

With everything in mind, it's not crazy to think I would be unrecognizable, a person with very different life path. I would probably leave my home much sooner, so there is a chance that before that I would be more independent — and therefore a little bit more detached from my family. But I'm sure that I would still hold more or less the same values since my family was normal and, luckily, free of any ethnic, racial, or sexual prejudices and discrimination.

Since we are on this topic, let me tell you about one situation where I truly felt like that boy inside of me came to the surface as a defense mechanism.

A Street Fight

Let me ask you something. When you sit at the dinner table, do you hold your hands under the table, or do you place your elbows on it, next to the plates and glasses? In my experience, women tend to do the first thing, they place their hands on their knees or just next to their bodies, while guys go elbow-up.

I have one more question for you. When you take off your shirt, do you take it off "the female way" — by crossing your hands, grabbing the bottom of your shirt on the opposite sides, and pulling it over your head, or do you use your collar to yank it over your head, which is what guys usually do? Well, I do what guys do, and this is also an unconscious action.

To be honest, when I sit, the only reason I cross my legs like most women is that I turned it into a habit a long time ago. I almost had to; society strongly advised it.

The point is, I was always a tomboy to a small degree, which is not surprising at all. And I was never ashamed of that in my pre-teen years because I was influenced by life's circumstances. None of my close friends found it weird; none of them made fun of me. What's more, they expected their friend Ivan would be just as available for fun times even though the name had changed.

It's not like I left them with pants on and returned in a dress.

What else do some boys do? They fight, and sometimes it can get pretty violent.

Now, I'm not saying this is a trait reserved only for males because I'm sure most of us have seen a few girl scraps, or we know some females that are always prepared for a rumble. But I think we can all agree that boys are just wired in ways that lean much more to physical violence. It was in our ancestors' DNA, and it's embedded in ours, too.

That mold actually escaped me because I had no desire to create enemies or to resort to a physical altercation. Actually, my closest friends were very peaceful, too, and we had lots of other ways of spending our energy. I can say with full confidence that we were pretty calm as a group.

But one day, trouble found me, and I guess Ivan had to take over for twenty minutes or so.

There was this one kid who came to our neighborhood late. As you might expect, he was looking to make new friends, and he tried to fit into our little gang. This is where things got a little complicated for him.

My buddies did nothing to the boy, but they did make things a bit harder for him. In other words, he had to show he fitted in before he could be considered a part of the team. I was not that much of a part of this, but my older friends did give him a tough time on several occasions.

I don't know if that was the reason that he went after me one night, but I wasn't gonna stand for it in any case.

We were shooting the hoops, some argument did start, I don't remember what about, and confrontation moved to the yard next to our improvised mini basketball court. He was pissed; he was ready to fight, so he clenched his fists as the desire to put one right in the middle of my face overtook his brain.

I did not want to get physical; he was bigger than me, but then he started to throw his hands, which were attempts I successfully avoided. After that, out of pure despair, he closed in on me and tried to trip me... several times. Unfortunately for him, I was aware of every attempt, and every time I managed to wiggle my leg out with little to no effort. As it turned out, that squiggly boy did not have much strength in his long limbs.

These efforts lasted for ten minutes or so, and he failed at absolutely everything. I was calm, but I do remember the blood rushing to my head at that point. At the same time, I heard nothing around me, like there were no people watching. I was hyper-focused on him, as I wanted to avoid any harm.

Never in my life did I return home with bruises on my face, and since I wasn't gonna start then, I observed his every unimpressive move.

He tried to trip me; I escaped. He tried to trip me again; I eluded once more. He was repetitive; he had no imagination or idea. At that point, things got pretty boring, so I decided to end it using his own method. I tripped him once, and he fell to the ground.

At that point, it was clear that the idea was not bad; the executor was.

This is where I had to make a decision — either I would let him get up, or I would hold him down. Since the first option would almost certainly lead to part two of this comical fight, and I had other things to do, I just held him down.

"Apologize, and I will let you up," I said to him.

"I apologize," he replied as he was getting calmer, and I moved so he could get back to his feet.

For me, the event ended right there, but my friends, who witnessed all of this, were not able to let it go that easily.

This fight was old news the next day, but they had their fun right after this boy had to admit defeat. They found it hilarious that he lost a fight to a girl, and they told him that, because of this fact, he needed to do twenty push-ups on the spot.

He did them, on the side of the road actually, and he told them, "Oh come on, guys, you know Ina and I are friends."

So, that was the only time I fought on the street, but I almost had a second confrontation, and this time it was his cousin. This just goes to show you that they were the problem, and not me.

His cousin didn't even live in our area, yet he felt the urge to attack me. He, like his cousin, got embarrassed, and this time it happened much quicker, with almost zero participation on my part. Gravity and poor judgment were his biggest enemies.

This is what happened, in short.

I walked home from school by myself, I minded my own business, I was about halfway to my house, and I heard my name being called. I turned around, and there he was, approaching me with bad intentions.

He started running towards me, he was getting closer, and it became quite clear that he was not just passing me by. So the second before he collided with me, I took a step to the left, I grabbed his shirt, and I slightly pulled it down so he could finish the downward spiral of his own momentum.

Another one bites the dust.

He was, too, bigger than me, and he was, I felt, more mean-spirited than the other one. But as luck would have it, an older person who saw the whole thing from a window started yelling at him, so he went home.

I can happily say these boys never picked on me again.

This was it, my entire combat history.

I don't need to fight; I don't want to fight. I'm not interested in spitting out blood or losing my teeth. But the funny thing is, nowadays, if someone would drag me into a girl scrap where some chick would pull my hair, I know for a fact I would not touch her hair. I would just use my fists, and this is where I, once again, return full circle.

Don't mistake me for a softy just because I don't practice violence, and I never saw any of my friends being attacked. If you attack me or someone I care about, that blood will know exactly where to rush.

The Unfair Advantage

During a period of about eight years, I covered MMA, mixed martial arts, mostly UFC, on a credible Croatian martial arts news website. I witnessed many great fights with male and female participants, and I even attended a few live events.

Before this job presented itself to me out of nowhere, I had little clue about the physical toughness of those remarkable, heavy-handed, hard-headed risk-takers. But it didn't take me long to realize how brutal this sport is, and I'm not only talking about the blood and the concussions. I am talking about the special level of toughness that these athletes need to possess in order to excel in this physical endeavor and unforgiving game.

If you are a fan of MMA, you might be familiar with one particular transgender athlete that was a popular topic in MMA news columns. I will not name any names.

She was a male most of her adult life, over thirty years, but after she went through gender reassignment surgery, she had several professional fights with female athletes. She did not have many pro bouts under her belt, but she did win most of them, and some wins were brutal.

This topic is maybe weirdly placed, and it may seem like it comes out of nowhere, but I feel like I have something to say about this since the debate was pretty heated at one point.

While reading about this, I couldn't help but imagine myself in this position. I even contacted one of the biggest athletic commissions in the USA to ask them if someone in my situation could compete in this sport, just out of curiosity. They confirmed to me that this possibility exists, but every presented case is treated individually.

Should this kind of competition be a thing? When it comes to a sport where people use their bodies and physical force to get a win, I say no.

The reason is simple.

I always felt like even me, a person with a female level of testosterone, on hormone replacement therapy, always had an advantage in strength and reaction time. I showed it in gym class. Now imagine a male going through sex change surgery at the age of thirty and then competing in weightlifting, boxing, fighting, or running against biological females.

Are we really so desperate to signal our progression that we are willing to sanction competition like this?

You are an adult, and you want to change your sex? Fine. You want to be accepted and not judged after you do so? Of course!

You are a transgender female, and you want to compete against biological women in a sport that can cause serious physical consequences? For whatever it's worth, I don't agree with that.

What I just said will not change anything, and I don't want it to. But if you are reading this and you are curios about my position, you now know where I stand. And even if this is on the way to becoming normal, I don't care. As we would say in Croatia, "This neither enters my pocket, nor leaves it."

If both parties engaged in a sanctioned fight are willing to scrap, go for it. But will I stand in its defence? I will not.

Chapter 9: To the People in My Boat

I've spent a lot of time in hospitals, and I've seen many ailing children. One thing I've never encountered, or maybe I did but never realized it, was a kid with a similar or same medical history as mine.

There are two main reasons for that. First lies in the fact that I've never gone out of my way to find him, her or them, and the other reason was an off-line life. No Google, no social media, no easy way to inform myself and connect with others.

Am I sorry I never tried to find a person like me and reach out? I can't blame myself or anyone else for this in retrospect because I remember what my stance was on this. I had absolutely no interest in regurgitating information and discussing the feelings I was trying to suppress. Get in, get out — this is what my trips to Zagreb looked like when I was visiting this city for medical checkups. Even the visits to local supermarkets after the fact were quick, because the sooner we were on that E3 highway, the more relaxed and happier I became.

Well, we live in different times now.

Information Technology

Because of all the technology we enjoy today, we have easy access to every single piece of information we need, and the bridge between ourselves and any other person in this world is not measured in miles any more. So if you are in my situation, I would like to think and hope that everything is a bit easier for you. The fact that I have the opportunity to write this book and a tool that will allow me to publish that same written work speaks, well, volumes.

I see young people that seem much more courageous than I was, and I think I know what was missing in my childhood — a rabbit hole. That's a hole people go into when they start investigating a subject on YouTube or any other website, and they can't seem to stop as new information is popping up just when they think they've seen everything.

The positive thing about the rabbit hole is that you can investigate it alone, without distractions or potential feelings of shame. In our case, we can find out on our own that there are people to turn to and that things aren't as dark as they seem. Once you realize that, this positive step can encourage you to actually reach out to somebody and talk to them face to face.

Shutting everybody out is maybe the most common thing kids do, and misinformation is only one of the harmful side effects. False or inaccurate information was, personally, the biggest pain in my ass. And this happened by sharing almost no facts with people around me.

When you share too little or nothing at all, other children's imaginations will fill in the blanks, and then you have an even bigger problem. They know, and yet they don't know. They are curious, so they will more likely ask somebody else. And after they find out something from a person that got informed by talking to some other uninformed friend, well, you have a huge mess on your hands, with only two options in front of you. Either you let the rumors spread, or you just speak up and share some actual facts.

Believe me, facts are always the right option because not long after you've done so, the story will become old news, and you will suddenly stop being the subject of conversation.

Be a straight shooter, feed curiosity with facts, and your life will become much easier.

Independence

Independence is important, even when it comes to regular checkups. If there is an opportunity for this, go do those checkups by yourself.

Of course, if you are a younger teenager, you most certainly won't wander around those maze-like hallways. But when the doctor calls your name, leave your parents in the waiting room, and visit the doctor alone. This will have some small but significant benefits for your psyche. This is you, slowly but surely, becoming an independent person. Take my word for it.

Years after that, you will think about moving to some other location, away from your home, which brings me to another crucial point. It's important to realize that you will no longer be surrounded by the people who know you or know about you. So it's a good thing to have a strategy about the proper way and time to come out.

I believe that if you are good friends with someone, they should know the real you. Their value in your life qualifies them and gives them the right to know. So when you feel that the time has come, go for it. Take that weight off your shoulders and get rid of it. You've had it long enough.

If you can't initiate the conversation face to face, initiate it through text and follow through with a one-on-one. I promise, once you break the ice, it will become much, much easier.

There are no guidelines on the best way to do this. Just do it however you feel is right, but make sure you do it. If that person is a true friend, they will read your message once, twice, maybe three times to process it, they will go past that initial surprise, and they will react with understanding and love. Mark my words.

The Benefit of the Doubt

You are, all in all, a normal person, but you are not an average human being. You are different, so don't judge people based on their initial surprise reaction.

Surprise is the default state for this kind of revelation. There's no other way around it; that's an undeniable fact. Give people some time to process this information because they have to compute something that is not that insignificant. You were one person to them two days ago, they are sure they know plenty about you, and this huge twist comes out of nowhere. But once they figure out where exactly to store this info inside the folder with your name on it, rest assured everything will click back to its place.

Not only that, but there's a good chance that bonds will be even stronger.

This is what happened in my situation, and it's obvious to me why that occurred. Before I came out, I had to hold everything in, but when you have it bottled up, it affects you, maybe even without you realizing it. I was told by several friends that they had the feeling I was hiding something, and only then did I notice how telling some of my behavior was.

It turned out I was subconsciously screaming out my admission, yet the speakers were not plugged in. Now this book is my biggest output.

The Victim Cards

I was once a sick child, but I managed to lead a fairly normal life. My cognitive abilities were not impaired, and I had no other disabilities, either. If this is you, too, listen up closely.

If you ever feel like you should get more from your family just because you suffered in the early stages of your life, you might feel tempted to ask for more or accept more if more is already offered; if that is the case, you should do yourself a favor and accept none of the extra, or just start with accepting half and work consciously to accept less as time passes.

More stuff and more attention sound good, but if your worst days are far behind you, you should empty your sleeves, give up your victim cards and just be an equal part of your family and society. Remember, you have suffered through enough, and nobody can take that away from you, but if you play these cards, you are becoming a victim all over again. Only this time, you are the casualty of your own miserable self-pity.

Also, you should think about the people who actually need to give that extra. If you have healthy siblings, two things can happen — either they will suffer because your parents sacrificed the attention reserved for them to be able to fulfill your supposed needs, or your parents will continue to give them their maximum attention, which will mean that increase in your needs will throw your parents into overdrive.

Imagine they gave one hundred percent, but now they will have to find an extra twenty percent to please you. They will most probably do it because love pushes people over those limits, but this is the time where you should think about the long-term consequences.

This is not good for them, and in the end, it's also bad for you.

Just give your parents a break; I certainly tried to do that. Sure, sometimes, my sister had the feeling that our old folks were more lenient with me, but facts painted a different picture in my case. On most occasions, my parents simply had no reason to get mad at me. I was a good, humble, well-mannered kid. I almost never asked for money, I never skipped classes, I never smoked, and I never got into any trouble. More often than not, I ruffled no feathers and caused no headaches, and when my sister did, she received the backlash, and then she identified it as an injustice.

That is, too, understandable.

Parental Advisory

I don't have my own kids, obviously. And I don't have sixty years in my rear-view mirror and tons of colorful life lessons that would qualify me to advise you on various important subjects. But my life is not completely lacking substance, and I feel like my lessons are about quality and not quantity.

So when I look back at my life, I feel the urge to speak up. My goal is to underline the stuff that was done right, as well as the issues I identified as problems.

I think one of the most important things is expressing emotions. This is more than just having a safety valve. This means letting your emotions out way before the pressure increases to a less stable level, and parents play the main role here.

If only a small part of this can be positively influenced by example, it should be fully taken advantage of. How open people are depends on more factors than just their upbringing, but there is no doubt a child can be positively influenced when it comes to sharing their feelings.

If I had my own family, "I love you" would not be something that is never said out loud because "it goes without saying." I would also strive to be a parent that discusses all the small issues with their kid. Because of this, when more delicate problems come along, there would hopefully be far fewer issues, resistance, and shame.

In my family, we cared for each other, and every single thing we had — we shared. My mother and I also discussed things when I was much younger, but unfortunately, I had no practice of talking to individuals outside my closest circle. This was something unforeseeable to my folks because I showed no signs of problems.

When it comes to shying away from true emotions, moms and dads can be even worse than kids. Luckily, I grew up in a normal environment, but I've seen some pretty uninvolved, uninterested, and preoccupied parents over the years.

The truth is, kind words said out loud won't make your throat sore, tears will not make your eyes burn, and one or two hugs a week will not chip anything away from that rock you represent.

And how about that sweet liberty?

Freedom is not an easy thing to give, but it's much easier when you are dealing with a teenager that does not hide a bunch of information from you. If your kid fills you in on important stuff and you listen and respond with good advice, you can more easily reward your child with more and more freedom as time passes. If you do that, this young person probably won't make important life moves in the future without consulting you first.

When it comes to saying no, your stance should be as strong as your love for that person. Even if your child has a harsh medical history, don't drastically change that approach if your kid is, in reality, physically and mentally fully capable of dealing with normal life challenges.

Don't let those issues be a rock in their shoes.

And if his or her illness is debilitating, of course, you will be there for them every step of the way.

Prepare Your Child for the Battle

Kids can be cruel or can say and do stuff that seems that way.

You can't always protect your child, and there's not much you can do to influence the behavior of other kids, but what you can do is prepare your daughter or son as best as you can for this journey and give them confidence. If your kid is well-liked and popular among his friends, that's an automatic plus for absolutely everything in his or her life.

That's why I like Jordan Peterson's advice, where he says that every parent's goal should be to make their kids likable and acceptable. Other kids should want to play with them, and other parents should like them. This is, in my opinion, absolutely spot-on.

We instinctively strive for a sense of belonging, and we feel incomparably better when we have it.

Fly, Fly Birdie

I've made it quite obvious in this book that this whole moving out thing was torture for me before things flipped in my head overnight. I understand that for many, leaving home is a long-awaited event, but for me, for the longest time, it was a nightmare I wanted to avoid.

Unfortunately, this is one more case where my objection to action turned out to be a huge waste of time and a road to nowhere. With that in mind, I want to point out several things about this with the hope that it will help someone who struggles with the same problem.

What I am about to say is a claim that could make some of you say, "It's easier said than done." If you do, I don't blame you because I've been known to have the same reaction. But my hope is that these words will have at least more weight to them, simply because of everything you've seen so far throughout these pages.

That's why I am emphasizing this so late in this book. I wanted you to find me qualified enough to let me be a positive influence.

This happens to me every single time. I have a challenging task in front of me, and if the solution doesn't seem straightforward to me from the start, I overestimate its complexity and underestimate my ability to solve it. It's similar with the moving — I magnified all the issues I could think of, I labeled them as impossible to solve, and I concluded that it's better to stick to a problem I can handle.

What a disservice!

We, as human beings, are remarkably adaptable. Many times, when we decide to take on a challenge, we end up laughing at the fear that we felt over the issue that, in the end, turned out to be relatively easy to overcome. Well, maybe it was not easy, but it was not unsolvable, either.

Just think about the first month of a new job. Every task you are supposed to handle on a daily basis seems to have more weight to it. The sheer volume of work seems too hard to handle, and people who are doing it with their eyes closed look like medal-deserving superhuman geniuses to you. One month in, most people end up with the same conclusion — it's not that bad.

Young people who have problems in social situations and hide in their comfort zones more often than not don't realize that only two weeks, three weeks, or a month would have to pass before they conclude that going solo into the world is not nearly as terrifying as they thought it would be. The same goes for the job — first, you learn, then you start to flow, and after that, you know so much that you become a teacher to new or less experienced colleagues.

Of course, you will encounter problems you failed to predict, but these issues will simply become yet another puzzle to solve in this game called life.

Closed Minds in Modern Times

I would like to think that we, as people, are a little more educated in the twenty-first century, where almost every single piece of information is just a click or two away. We have everything at our fingertips, and luckily, the best sources of information and common sense receive more and more attention.

A good example is the UFC commentator and stand-up comedian, Joe Rogan, with his podcast, as well as clinical psychologist Jordan B. Peterson with his big worldwide tours. I have to place Sam Harris in the same intellectual company, too, as well as Richard Dawkins. I mention them in the same breath because some of them don't agree on many issues, and yet they are capable of having civil conversations about it. They are very inspiring!

Unfortunately, some people are stuck with all kinds of prejudices. Maybe "stuck" is not even the right word for it because it's not forced upon them. They could learn to let it go, especially if somebody they care about is directly affected by their outdated mindset.

Luckily, it seems like the tides are shifting in a positive manner in many parts of the world, but there are still plenty of people who cannot accept things like homosexuality and gay marriages.

I cannot relate to many of the issues, I can't call myself a victim, but I can say something about being different.

My hope is that everyone realizes that you are what you are as far as sexual preferences go. You cannot truly reprogram a person, a child, or an adult, either with meditation or medication. Just look at my situation, and everything will become clear. I did not produce any "extra" testosterone for twenty-five plus years, I have been on hormone replacement therapy for more than eighteen years, and my fundamental software has not changed at its core.

Let's stop pretending like we can rearrange ones and zeros in this binary code of human existence. Whatever the situation is, you just have to deal with it and accept it.

I will be on hormone replacement therapy for the rest of my life because of justified reasons. Hormonal balance is important, and test results showed multiple times that some of my levels are normal for a female person of my age, which is a sign that those pills are doing their job. That was, after all, the goal because the medical condition demanded as much. Also, I have no delusions about the role female hormones have had in shaping me, both physically and psychologically.

But this is where meddling with my software stops. This is, actually, the only software I have because that chromosome issue had to be addressed in some manner early in my life.

What disturbs me are people who try to alter a healthy child's mind just because they can't accept their sexuality. What saddens me are the consequences that a young person suffers, no matter if medications are included or not. If you have a kid that struggles with these issues, you don't have to do much to push him or her deeper into a state of desperation. So this is risky territory, even more nowadays, because of social media.

So please, teach your child good life values, help your child navigate through this crazy world, but try to mess with their compass as little as possible. And if you have any prejudice, I'm happy to tell you that this issue actually is something that can be altered. It just takes time, understanding, and some goodwill. You can do it. Everybody can.

How sad is it to see parents kicking their gay kid out after finding out the truth? How unfortunate is it to see parents becoming desperate as they receive early hints that their kid's sexual preferences may not be what they hoped for, so they try to sway them in the preferred direction in all kinds of ways? And how depressing is it to see children who try to hide in the closet from the very people who should love them for what they are?

It's very disturbing to me, and the other extreme bothers me, too. Unfortunately, there are cases where parents place their six- seven- or eight-year-old kid on hormone replacement therapy just because their child claims their mind and their body don't match.

This is where parenting fails too, as these decisions should be made by a much more developed brain. As far as I'm concerned, it's better to wait than to grant this kind of wish this early, for obvious reasons.

Bullying

The day I reflected on my teenage days and concluded that I was never systematically bullied was the day I truly comprehended the destructive nature of the act of bullying itself.

Despite what you might think, based on the story you've learned, I was pretty much spared. In a way, you can attribute the bad stuff that happens to a person to the vulnerability that somebody projects. It's unfortunate, but that's the way it is sometimes — the more you look like prey, the higher the chances are you're going to get stalked, jumped, and chewed up.

Me, I had the potential to be a real victim, but I had the fortune to grow up in a peaceful area and around normal people. Physical violence in school hallways was something I only saw in TV series and movies. The same goes for clichéd bully verbal attacks and ruthless, repetitive picking on a single individual. As a matter of fact, when I was nine or ten, if you asked me if I thought that was something that happens in real life, I would have probably said no.

But the movie scenes are not exactly exaggerated. Somewhere, sometime, for someone, the reality is much more horrible than the pictures that try to paint a realistic view of this harmful behavior. For some people, the battles are daily and lost in advance, and the war seems infinite. After that realization, I was no longer surprised that so many kids suffer from a lack of confidence and depression.

What if I had encountered that level of brutality in my youth? I can only speculate about the things that happen in some other, imagined reality, but I can't envision myself being here to write this book. Somebody would have to tell my story for me, but the problem is, the only two people who would be able to tell it would, as it seems, be gone.

But I was, all in all, left alone. The kids that made me uncomfortable left it that way and pushed no further, and friends that appreciated me felt that way regardless of my nature. My family was there, too, and that meant that almost every single ounce of negative energy in my life had a fit counterpart, which held me in a pretty stable balance throughout my life.

I know exactly how it is to end up deep down in the dumps, despite the fact there were not that many deadly bullets to dodge. So how did I manage to get back up? One thing that got me motivated was thinking about this life as a one-time deal that it actually is. Life is not a Nintendo console, where the reset button will give you another crack at it.

So for me personally, I always felt like there was too much effort given for all of this to be thrown away. You know that feeling when you put enough puzzle pieces in place, and you think that you've come too far to take everything apart and place it back in the box? That's where I am on my best days. When the sun shines the brightest, this becomes my way of thinking. I worked too hard to just give up. And when depression kicks in, I try to regain that feeling.

I really wish that one day bullying will become too insignificant in the number of cases to even be included in any statistics. It is tragic because of the fact it's so pointless and yet so dangerous. If any bully reads this book, I want you to reevaluate your actions because the last thing you want is to find a victim in a similar state to what I was in.

You don't want this person on your conscience.

Chapter 10: The Finish Line

My mom passed away in 2016. I was twenty-seven years old. Was I ready to write a book back then? Maybe, but book writing never crossed my mind three or four years ago. To be fair, this was an idea born a few hours before I started to place some ideas on paper.

Now, my mom is no longer here, and with her, a huge part of my story is gone, too. The sadness I felt after she left went more or less dormant in 2017, but writing this book made my sorrow reemerge, partially because I have so many questions to ask her.

I don't know what I was thinking, Mom. I had you by my side all those years, and it never occurred to me to revisit and review my early life experiences with you as an adult.

What happened to me? As a seven-year-old child, I talked to my friends about my situation. I borderline bragged about it if someone asked me if everything was real. And I was never scared to ask questions. But after the second and third grades, that brash kid was taken down, any trace of confidence was wiped out, and in one year, I went from being crazy in the hallways to one of the quietest kids in class.

Now I am left with only part of the narrative, and I wish you were here so I could read this to you because you would add so much to the story I am trying to share with the world. And I wish you were here so I could see your reaction to me moving to Zagreb.

I would show you the apartment, introduce you to my friends, and this would be the first time I would drive *you* to Croatia's capital, a city I once hated. Who knows, maybe you would take a nap in the car part of the way, just as I did every time we drove here, on early Monday mornings. This time our safety would be in my hands, I would be the one solving problems, and you would be the one lying back and taking in your surroundings.

You depended on those dialysis machines for twenty years, and for such a long time, we depended on you. So this chapter is dedicated to you and to all the important people in my life.

Appreciation and Acknowledgment

Life isn't something that is cherished enough by most people, and it seems like it's taken for granted more often than not. But boy, we are grateful when someone saves it, aren't we?

Let's imagine this scenario. You are walking on the edge of a cliff. You are not trying to die, but you figure that the closer you get, the greater the view must be. Then you suddenly feel dizzy, you lose your balance, and to your horror, the fall into the abyss seems inevitable. But in a split second, people behind you, who were happy and fulfilled enough with the view they've been getting a few feet back, grab you and stop you from plummeting over that edge.

You didn't even realize they were behind you, and they just saved your ass.

How would you feel about those people? My guess is that you would do anything for them from that point on, right?

The little picture I've been trying to paint above describes a part of my life because, on several occasions, I did feel like I was on my metaphorical edge. And just like that "cliff hanger" was grateful he had people around him when he needed them the most, I am thankful for the human beings that grabbed me by my shoulders just at the right time.

The funny thing is, they don't even realize they did it, so I will have to tell them, and what better way to end this book. This is a small but, hopefully, worthy tribute to all the important people in my life. All of these individuals and groups of people, who will not be named separately, contributed in some way to my sanity. Some of them even saved my life at this stage that I am in now.

The Original Line-up

First and foremost, I am thankful for my earliest childhood friends, a very special group of boys, as they were the first ones in my hometown to be introduced to the new me. I thank you guys because "new me" was, in fact, the "old me" in your eyes, and in a world where kids were judging, digging, and whispering, you were a sanctuary I always returned to.

You helped me to be free, you've shown me how to be brave, outgoing, and open. You never excluded me, and I always felt protected. At the same time, I feel sad when I think about how we are not in contact any more, but I guess this is what happens when life takes people on completely different paths.

On certain days, I spent more time with you than with my family, so you were my second family. There is no sport we didn't improvise with, from soccer on bumpy, rough, and uneven fields, to basketball on a homemade court and baseball with shitty wooden sticks.

We had the whole neighborhood to ourselves, and we made it our playground. We played smart, and at times we played stupid and dangerous, but we were still sharp enough to stay safe. We shared so much in common, and I was so lucky I had you in one of the most challenging periods of my life.

On the opposite side, I had a girl team, a group of girls I am in contact with today.

Girls, you knew fewer details about my situation because you are younger than me, and we never talked this out. But you are all one of those truly special human beings who made me feel loved and accepted. A big part of all this is your parents, too, who accepted me and loved my mother as well.

Countless hangouts and birthday parties that go back as far as I can remember are kept, cherished, and are immortal. I am happy knowing there are plenty of them to come.

Not that I care if people hang out more with men or women, or they have that evenly spread, but I really felt like I needed a female group in my life because you helped me find my balancing point in that sense early on. I never had any fears about the future of our friendships, and even my doubtful mind has no doubt that all of you feel the same.

If you need anything, and I mean *anything*, ever, and I can provide it, just call me, and I will be ready to deliver.

Friendship Lottery Win

My dad plays bingo often, and every time he prepares for it, he repeatedly dreams of the things he would do with the winnings. After that, if Lady Luck avoids him and if she visits Zagreb instead, which happens suspiciously often but, in reality, is perfectly normal because of the number of players from his city, he gets annoyed.

While Dad was matching randomly drawn numbers with the numbers on his card, I was playing my own lottery, and Zagreb was really the winner. This was a different game, though, the stakes were much higher, and I truly feel like I've walked away with millions.

I was offered the chance to come to Zagreb before I actually arrived, several times, and my reply was an instant no. No rethinking, zero chance of accepting. The fears that poisoned my brain had more weight to them than the potential benefits of the move, and I simply refused.

Knowing how my brain works, I knew what I had to do — I just needed to let my imagination run wild. When I really want something, my brain quickly thinks of the many scenarios from the very beginning, and I get worked up about it way too early. Often this kind of emotional investment leads to feelings of disappointment if you fall short.

So this is what changed — I let myself think of the Zagreb scenario for the first time since I was offered the chance to move there. Right there and then, I imagined all the good sides of the move, I ignored the potential bad parts, and I asked my boss if the offer still stood. He said yes. I took a deep breath, and a few weeks later, I packed my suitcase.

I really didn't have any clue what to expect because even though I had the most experience in this firm, I was not actually a part of the team since I worked from home. Now I was physically joining a group of people I didn't know, and I knew there was a chance I would be considered an intruder.

Despite that, finally, I arrived.

In the beginning, I was quiet and careful, in my default state, but I was giving myself a break on this one because one giant step for my-kind was made. The firm had over twenty people employed at that time, after all, so the reactions to my arrival varied a little. But overall, nobody was mad. I was present, and my two main goals at that point were to show gratitude by doing a good job and to show my colleagues I came in peace.

Move forward several years, and I am a much richer person. Richer in job and life experience, and richer in friends.

The job was not easy, it was a pressure cooker at times, but as far as interpersonal relationships go, something great happened. These amazing human beings were the ingredients of a truly one-of-a-kind recipe that is hard to recreate. I don't know where all of this came from, how these different personalities ended up in the same pot, but something extraordinary did happen.

I know that because, in this particular work environment, our bond was tougher than the times we were in.

I was always very tempted to reveal everything about myself to you. I'm sorry I was not brave enough to do it earlier, so consider this book to be, at least in part, a manifestation of the courage you helped me gain.

All I ever wanted for myself was to be chain-free, not to be dragged down and destroyed by the knowledge that I have to come out with my life story every time someone new enters my life. I had the keys all along, and the lock opened the second this book entered the consciousness of the people around me.

You are my family number three, so I am, as it happens, extremely lucky and wealthy. Your capacity to care and love is truly big and something I strive for, and I hope I am just as good of a friend to you.

Last but Not Least

I know how it feels to work all day, every day, on weekends, too — the batteries run out, days off are not enough to charge them, and exhaustion builds up. Now multiply that by ten, and this is there; I am no longer able to imagine how one person can do their job under these kinds of conditions and for a longer period of time.

My dad did exactly that. He was working his ass off for thirty-plus years for his family. From Monday to Saturday, he would leave at seven a.m. and return at about seven p.m. His was a physically demanding job. Mentally too, because of the possibility of falling from a roof or a building and instantly killing himself.

I am lucky I have my dad, and I was fortunate to have my grandparents in my life, too. I can't finish this book without mentioning my sister, my aunt, my uncle, my cousin, my niece, and her father, also.

I failed to mention some, but you should all know that you all made my life a whole lot richer. If we ever talked and laughed together, you became a piece in this mosaic I call "A life worth living."

A Person That Deserves Her Own Book

What can I say about my mom? She gave birth to me, and she cared for me. She was there to receive the news that her child was sick. She gave me everything, her time, her love. She cried when she had to leave me at the hospital for the first time, she made me feel safe despite all the life drama, and she made sure that I never walked alone through all of my adversities.

Thank you, Mom, for giving me my freedom with my friends from my earliest childhood. Thank you for trusting me and for being in my life every step of the way. Thank you for putting me first even when your health was compromised and thank you for being harsh but fair with me when I made my mistakes.

You cooked, cleaned, worked around the house even when you weren't supposed to. You drove the family car for miles and miles for me despite the fact that your illness was always taking its toll. We were never worthy of you. We never did enough for you. I will be the first to admit it, even though I was the one that probably gave you the most in return.

You were so amazing and strong that for many years I wasn't even conscious about the severity of your health condition. You inherited your strength from your mother, and when I go back to these chapters to reread them, a very positive thought comes to mind — maybe I inherited at least a part of that strength myself.

Maybe this realization ends up being the most important product of this written work, who knows. Maybe this will help me to finally appreciate myself.

But I know one thing. Even if I never sell a single copy, these pages will always remain as a tribute to everything I went through and as a reminder of you. A sum of my thoughts, my best try so far to explain what I feel, and to underline the importance of your existence in our lives.

You sacrificed so much, you were sick, and you still had the strength to take care of the family and the time to play with me. My friends remember you fondly. They remember the awesome mom that had unbelievable patience with kids.

One of my first memories ever is of a backyard wrestling match with my friends. And where did we wrestle? In the circle in the yard that you made for us. Just as you marked that playground area, you marked a whole soccer playing field on the grass that you cut yourself, just so we could get our daily dose of fun.

When we wanted the company of a grown-up, you happily agreed to play cards or Monopoly with us, and when some of my friends needed help for some handmade project, you were delighted to help. You loved kids, kids loved you, and I truly can't comprehend where you pulled all that will, love and patience from, especially given the severity of your health issue.

I remember when you and I looked at each other moments after our car flipped over, a second before I jumped out of that car to try to call for help. I would relive and survive that with you a hundred more times if that meant I could spend more time with you. Even if I knew that the one hundred and first time would be final for us, I would still pick that.

I was fully aware you were sick, but I still didn't think that six months after this car crash, you would be gone. A few days before you died, you were in unbearable pain all day, and you still didn't cry. I'm sorry I didn't do more when the final emergency came; I wish I had been calmer and more collected in that critical moment; maybe that would have saved you, and maybe that would have given your life an extra year or two.

But I heard something very wise from Jordan Peterson, and I really think it's thoughtful and precise. Would I put this exact blame on some other person, a family member, if they had done what I did in that situation? I most certainly would not. I would tell that person that he or she did the best he or she could in those circumstances.

So with that being said, maybe I should stop torturing myself.

In the end, when I think about it, maybe that was the way it was supposed to be. You were there when I came into this world, and I was there when you left it. Together, from the beginning to the end.

The Importance of Positive Influence

Ever since I can remember, I passively lived through every situation my mom had to go through.

When the money situation was poor, and she had to figure out what to do, I was there worrying with her. I couldn't help it. When she was paying the bills, I was there next to her, so I continued to do that myself later on. I was so conscious about our financial situation that when she often wanted to buy me something, I stopped her from doing it if I thought we needed the cash more.

This was a result of my closeness with my mom. Any move she made, I was there, standing on her feet and doing life's dance along with her.

My family is certainly not perfect, but it was perfectly normal. My father showed me enough love, I didn't lack it, but he was working long hours, so you cannot compare this with the closeness I had with my mother. My grandmother, on my mother's side, was another big positive influence in my life.

I was surrounded by pretty tough and well-respected people. Granny had rheumatic arthritis for thirty years, yet despite having every single bone deformed and being dependent on crutches ever since I remember, she worked in her garden and went to the market up until the age of eighty-two. People loved and respected her, as they did her husband, my grandfather, who succumbed to illness ten years before she died, when I was nineteen.

I can certainly point to several other people, but I don't have to. The point is clear; I have people to look up to. It's on me now to have at least half of the positive influence that my mom, my grandmother, and my grandfather did. They differed from one another, especially Grandfather, but they had something in common — love in their hearts and people's respect.

It's such a tragedy to lose these sorts of people, but it's such a fortune to have these kinds of human beings to lose. Instead of thinking about the tragedy of the loss, I'd rather think about the luxury of having known them and spending my youth alongside them.

Feat of Strength

They say pain is the one constant in life, and I believe them. They also say that in order to be meaningful, life requires pain, as it is the main motivator and the fuel for everything worthwhile that we do during our existence. Well, considering the amount of pain, my life should be pretty meaningful. Also, I know for a fact that, against the odds, I did go through psychological growth during my most challenging periods.

I had just enough of a balance to avoid blowing my brains out. All the happiness in my childhood kept me sane, while all the painful moments I had to confront made me just a bit stronger and prepared me for inevitable shitstorms.

What I want to say to everyone is, these storms are something to be prepared for, not something to be avoided because you can't avoid them for the rest of your life. It will only boomerang on you, but this time it will be bigger and mixed with an all-new set of flying debris.

So envision yourself wearing a raincoat and not an invisibility cloak. You are tough because you are here despite your worn-out shoes and wet socks. And walk with your head high because that's the only way you can spot and find the things you desire.

I am thankful that your field of vision was wide enough to spot my book, and I truly hope I did fulfill your expectations with its substance.

Thank you for becoming a part of my life story.

Shoutout to my Intellectual Influencers

I am by no means an expert on any particular subject, nor do I pretend to understand most of the stuff I hear on podcasts and documentaries I regularly consume. But I have this irresistible urge to dose myself with information in subjects I'm attracted to, and I do so with a hope that every single time I listen to something, at least one tiny fraction of it will rub off on me.

I don't know if I should brag about this or state it with a sense of shame, but I will admit it: most of the books I listened to – and I listened to many in the past few months – are too complicated for my full understanding, and I should probably revisit them more than once. This goes for many podcast episodes, too.

You will probably guess some of the books that are in my Audible library by the names I'm about to mention, and if you do, you will also probably know why I struggle with the content. Nevertheless, I want to mention these people, as they are a part of my healthy brain diet. They are my "Omegas" of the podcast and YouTube worlds, and with them, I balance out the unhealthy "sugars" and "carbs" that are readily available and very tempting to weak minds.

I will not go into depths here, as I just want to tell the world about authors and podcasters whose content I'm in love with. This is a shout-out to the late and great American Carl Sagan, who was made of elements forged in stars that specifically wanted to create a poet who will speak about their creation in the most amazing and infatuating ways. If you wish to discover or deepen your love for the universe, just read some of his books, or look at some of his presentations and interviews on YouTube. That will light the spark and do the trick.

One other science communicator I love to listen to is Neil deGrasse Tyson, who, in many ways but in his own style, continued where Carl left off. He has a presence on all channels, so whether you want to learn more about our cosmos through books, or on the podcast

StarTalk, he is your man. *StarTalk* is a show I would recommend to everybody, as its brilliant merge with comedy – brought to you largely by Chuck Nice – makes learning extra fun.

Who else do I enjoy listening to? British evolutionary biologist Richard Dawkins, whose atheism versus religion debates can be extra spicy and fun, and Sam Harris, a neuroscientist with ideas about free will that will make you think hard about it – whether you can help it or not. And if these geniuses happen to be on the same panel, it's an early Christmas for me!

It seems like I place a new name on my list on a weekly basis, like theoretical physicist Brian Greene with his *World Science Festival* six months ago, or computer scientist and AI researcher Lex Fridman even more recently. You can see the pattern now more or less, for sure, as many of them crossed each other's' paths on at least one occasion.

Internet brings them together and makes them available to us, and not many individuals do a better job at stirring that melting pot than Joe Rogan, former *Fear Factor* star with polarizing presence in UFC, stand-up comedy, and podcasting. The JRE podcast has become the top stop for all kinds of characters, with pretty much any kind of back story and profession you can imagine.

I can go on and on, but this is the time to stop, as I think I painted a good picture or what sources tickle and scratch my curiosity. The fact that *Joe Rogan Experience* podcast episodes helped me greatly just days after my mother's death is "enough said". I'm so fortunate I was clear-minded enough to press play every time I was alone in the months following this chain of events. I found my therapy when I needed it the most and I'm sure even Joe would say that the source, in this case, was very unlikely.

So I say to all these people – I am thankful for your unlikely existence!

The Indelible Trail of a Deceased Loved One

Over time, the images in our thinking machines become fainter and grainier. Like technology in reverse, the resolution loses the number of pixels, all the way back to a point where we can't even assign colors or sounds to the faint visual outlines we are left with.

But somehow, the feelings are left preserved. They can be triggered by a memory, photograph, or even a smell, and this made me a trigger-happy person many times in my life.

With my mother being gone since 2016 and her being very sick for twenty years prior to that, I have to reach way, way back in the past if I want to remember something from the time when health issues weren't "hanging around our necks like some two-tone medallion" (shout-out to David Jason/Del Boy from *Only Fools and Horses*). I don't have much to work with, as I was barely seven in 1995, but every single piece of treasure I possess holds its value in a currency called "feelings" even today.

The feelings are deep; they pass through the body — guts first, and they exit in the form of goosebumps, and as long as I dedicate a few minutes of my time to reminisce, the feel-good cycle continues.

The earliest memories of my mother are almost always placed in fall or winter ambiance, with the wind blowing, leaves flying around us or even snow falling, with the sun shining ever so softly. But I am as cozy and warm as I've ever been.

I am a small figure walking next to a larger shape that represents the center of my gravity and the main source of my warmth and happiness. No matter how cold it was or where we were, I internally and undeniably knew that I was following the best footsteps one could hope for. The kindness she had was a magnet that drew other people in, and the natural internal and external beauty she possessed radiated from her like light from a newborn star.

How lucky I was to have my mother for all those years, and how lucky I am to possess all these memories now.

Many of us have experienced tough losses in our lives, as they are painfully inevitable and often too bitter to swallow. But for those of us whose lives continue to go on, we have a duty to guard these memories and create new ones. Because one day, we will be a collection of pixels in someone else's thinking machine, and the more important question will be — what kind of feelings are they accompanied by?

The Aftermath

This book was not my secret project. Actually, it was partially imagined as a power tool I will use for anything that is screwed up in my life. The second I started with it, I couldn't wait to share the idea with my friends, but before I could do that, I had to work on my strategy carefully.

My main issue was, of course, the fact that almost nobody in Zagreb knew my life story, so I had to be careful. The purpose of this book is also to rediscover my freedom, but I could only guess about the price and potential repercussions of my move.

So to avoid any harm or at least to minimize the risk, I coined the plan that looked like this.

First, I will hint to my friends I am writing a book, which will, without a doubt, spark further interest and questions. Second, I will answer some of the queries, but when my friends ask me about the theme of the book, I will tease them with it so that I can buy myself some time. During that time, I will work on the introduction, and I will send it to them while crossing my fingers and hoping for the best.

This is precisely what I did. The introduction you see at the beginning of this book was the text I shared with other people, some of whom knew something about my story and many of whom knew nothing.

My instincts were right. The move turned out to be a smart one, and reactions were positive. More than that, they were better than I could have hoped for.

Of course, people were surprised, I mean, who wouldn't be, but support was one hundred percent there, which warmed up this beating rock I have in the middle of my chest. The messages were truly something to be seen. As a matter of fact, they were almost overwhelming to me.

I received two important confirmations from this. Number one: It reinforced my notion that life is worth living, which is something I needed to receive not just now, but a few times earlier in my life, too. Second: Every single friend told me, I hope with as little bias as possible, that the content of the introduction had quality and good substance. They described to me how it gripped them and made them want to read more, so this was my green light. I was fired up and ready to go.

But hold on, why would I tell people about my book before writing it, and I have no other similar writing experience? Good question! If everything seems ass-backward, you are right, but that's just the way I am — ass-backward.

I had no other choice in life, I did this, many times, and it's always better than the alternative. I rarely do some important things from the beginning, step by step. Instead, I always need to do some things that lock me in, otherwise it wouldn't be done.

One example is my move to Ireland, which ended up lasting only 4 months. But nevertheless, I went there by sacrificing a lot, and I threw my stuff out of my closet even before I 100% decided I will go. And after I did the stuff that marked the point of no return, I felt better because this is it — I'm going to Ireland!

Why did I do that? Because I knew I wanted to go and I had the ability to go, and I had to use some weapon against the fear that was creeping it.

I got wise, you see. I have found a solution for fear, and the same method was useful when I opened my sole trade business in Croatia, too. It's literally a message to my fearful side — *"There, I did it. What are you going to do about it?"*

Overdue, Overnight Maturation

After I pulled the biggest move of my life, and by that, I mean writing this book, I realized how easy the rest could be. People asked me some pretty delicate questions, and for the first time, I had the courage to answer them, and I did it with a smile on my face. The smile came as a result of their reaction because it was interesting to see the surprise on their faces as they were trying to find out more.

The introduction, after all, was a teaser, and this showed that it served its purpose.

To show you how messy my confessions were before this, I will tell you details about a recent one. To be fair, there were only a few of them altogether, so I had little practice.

This is what it looked like: I sent a text with the explanation while being as nervous as ever, and I turned the volume way down on my phone, so I would not receive the notification of the response. It took me about an hour to get myself to wake my phone up to see the preview of the message I had received. If I still had any alcohol left in me at the time, which I used for courage, it was gone by that point. Adrenaline just evaporated any traces of that beer.

My heart was pounding, I was terrified, and I kept thinking about the friendship I had potentially lost as a result of my admission.

In reality, I never lost anyone after sharing my story, which was a huge load off my back because I would hate to think, that the one thing I can't change about my life, is a dividing factor.

If you think this was bad, I can tell you that it was even worse before that. As a matter of fact, I had zero skills developed when it came to having an actual open conversation about the subject, even with my longtime friends. It turned out that this, too, required maturity.

In the end, the further I went outside my old comfort zone, the greater the reward was.

This book writing process turned out to be pretty cool because I am asking the questions I always wanted to ask out loud, and it looks like I have the answers to most of them. Who would have ever guessed it?

I'm looking to expand on this freedom I am feeling right now; I'm doing my best to get some wind under these clipped wings. I am sensing real possibilities for the first time, like something big and vital is actually on the horizon of my life, and I will attempt to catch this slow momentum and give it an extra push while it lasts.

I was scared, and now I am asking, "Afraid of what?" I was embarrassed, and now I am thinking, *Who gives a crap!* I was unwilling to discuss my situation with others, and now I say, "What would you like to know?"

There are plenty of things I do now that surprise me.

The Never-Ending Dilemma

One of my friends, who lives in another country, was also the receiver of my introduction. As a result of this, for the first time, he decided to ask me a few questions.

Up until that point, I was not even sure if he knew anything about this, but he revealed to me that he was told about my situation a long time ago, so he had an idea but not much more than that.

"So, are you a girl?" he asked me in person.

I told him, "Well, on paper—"

"No, I am not talking about the papers. I am asking you, are you a girl?"

I suppose he wanted me to express how I feel, as this is more important than anything else.

I said that I am, but I was reminded of how difficult it is to explain this issue to some people. You see, to you I am whatever you say I am.

How can I answer this question and be honest?

You can say I have no clue how it is to be a woman. Fair enough. But at the same time, you can also say that I don't know what it's like to be a man — because that's even truer. Maybe I know something about how it is to be a boy, but when you are five or six years old, how much of a difference is there, anyway?

So call me Ina, call me Ivan, call me what you want. Call me a man, a woman, or something in-between. What I'm not is a person who will be able to give a satisfactory answer to that question, and what I am is a human being.

People can accept me or avoid me in general. When somebody accepts me, I feel that much more enriched, happy, and fortunate. When the opposite happens, I recognize that, and at the same time, I hope that my life story was not the main reason.

It's easy to understand and accept the repercussions when you know you did something wrong. But if my story is the main reason for the fallout, the situation becomes a little harder to digest.

Because I kept most of my stuff to myself, I felt minimal backlash as a consequence of my medical history. Now the cards are on the table, and I'm going all-in.

Call me a risk-taker.

The Future

The book is coming to its end, and I've touched on almost everything except for my love life. The reason this part is missing from these pages is that it's missing from my life, too. Nothing ever happened that is worth mentioning, and by explaining further, I would only be regurgitating the same problems I've already mentioned in previous chapters. So I will only say this.

During my life, I've seen plenty of different doctors. Some of them saw me for the first and for the last time, simply because I was switching from place to place for various tests.

In that time frame, I noticed that many of them knew very little about my situation, so I would receive quick advice like, "When you are ready, you and your boyfriend can come here, and you can do this procedure." (I've mentioned this before).

I don't blame the doctors since they have many patients on their hands and plenty to worry about, but in this case, I was angry.

It seemed to me like I was listening to a person who thought that:

a) I have a boyfriend

b) I'm interested in boys

c) I wanted this sex change

I have to be honest with you, this was a bit annoying to me at the time, and I remember thinking:

a) I don't have a boyfriend

b) I'm not interested in boys

c) I didn't ask for this sex change

By the way, do these people even realize what this "boyfriend" would have to accept before entering into a relationship with me?

Along with this, I was thinking that, even if I was interested in boys, how in the world would I ever want to participate in sexual activity when my private regions have been paraded around hospitals, doctors' offices, and operating rooms for years? I can't count how many people have seen "me" by now, and you don't even want to know how many foreign objects were used on "me" by this point.

In all honesty, I've fought three lives' worth of battles.

I can't predict the future and don't know where I will be in five or ten years, but I just wanted to be clear that I am OK with any outcome. I'm not looking at other couples and jealously wishing I was in their shoes, and I try not to look at relationship status as a measurement tool when defining myself or anybody else. Also, I don't dwell on the fact that I can't have biological kids.

My life is moving right now, it is not standing still, so at least I have one condition needed for good things to happen in the future. I still have my moments, I can still go from a hundred miles an hour to a low-energy period of one or two days when I feel more down and susceptible to depression, but it's far from being debilitating.

In some other scenario, these pages would not exist, and who knows, maybe the book would be a posthumous publication. But it's not. It's one win for me.

Bring it, Life, I'm standing right here. Your troubles made me do this. I'm exposing all of my difficulties, stresses, and struggles and repurposing every single ounce of pain as fuel. Every shitty memory is being redeployed, so, Crap, meet your alternative use-value.

Fingers crossed I make it.

Bonus Material Ahead

Technical Specification

Throughout this book, I tried to stay away from biology and medicine. It's not that I think it would be too much for my readers, not at all — it's just that I don't have a clue about half of these things myself, so why pretend.

But I can't avoid it, neither would I want to, so instead of randomly sprinkling blurry information, I decided to dedicate one tiny part to all things medical. This realization arrived late, and it came thanks to my dear friends, who started asking questions I couldn't provide full answers to. This outcome is logical, but since logic is not always my thing, I ended up adding these paragraphs right in the middle of my quiet, internal celebration of "finishing" this book.

Of course, I wouldn't be able to do this myself since my medical notes are made up of dozens and dozens of brief, often repetitive, and hard to understand information, so I asked my doctor for some help. He agreed to provide it, which I'm very grateful for, so I present you with some extra information about my medical history.

This will not be long, but it will be the information you will seek if you are curious like my buddies are. Also, this is important to every human being who is in the same boat, and reading this book, because this way you can make your comparisons and connections. There are, after all, many variations to most medical conditions, and this one is no different.

So it goes like this.

At an earlier stage, an exploratory laparotomy was performed, a surgical procedure that opens the abdominal cavity to examine the organs located in the abdomen. In a series of examinations in the period before the final surgery, a left undeveloped gonad was found, while the right testicle was proclaimed "immature" (it did not fully develop).

In the same ballpark, time-wise, a hypoplastic (small and underdeveloped) uterus was discovered, which many years later was not even visible on one of the ultrasound examinations. "Pseudopenis" is also mentioned in my medical records, which, depending on the case, is often described as a penis-like formation or enlarged clitoris. It was explained to me that they both develop from the same embryonic basis.

I was faced with a lot of inquiries after I came out, and one of the main ones was this: Why was six the age at which the surgery was performed? Why six and not four, five, or ten? This is very difficult to answer.

With the help of medical professionals, my parents had to decide how to correct the genitals and what path to choose for a kid with a gender differentiation disorder. As my original doctor said, attitudes about it vary, and they've certainly changed over the years.

And what about that tumor I've previously mentioned (I've referred to it as cancer my whole life)? In the case of a person with a gender differentiation disorder caused by chromosomal abnormalities, there is a risk of tumor development in problematic gonads, which is why removal is recommended.

As I've written about in this book, I have used hormone therapy for a long time, Estrofem tablets to be more precise, and I am stuck with them for the rest of my life. Those who know this are intrigued by the questions that bothered me too, for years. What happens if I stop taking Estrofem, they ask?

I was afraid to test it out, but the quick reply is the development of osteoporosis and breast reduction. No, I wouldn't grow a beard, and yes, my testosterone is as low as any other average female person of my age. For that testosterone, like the others, I have an adrenal gland to thank.

So this is it. As far as I can tell, all the important info has been revealed. But just in case I did leave something out, and you wish to know more, feel free to e-mail me at info@inushdigital.com. Who knows, maybe your question will be a spark that lights up a section of my life that I mistakenly left alone in the dark, and a new chapter reveals itself.

Peace, Love, and Positivity

Life was never easy. We, as human beings, after all, did arrive at this point after millions of years of trial-and-error refinement. Life was not quick at this fundamental method of problem-solving, but it obviously got it done eventually, and now we have the consciousness and power to self-improve.

It looks to me like we are moving in a positive direction, which brings me to hope that generations in the not-so-distant future will live in a world with only a negligible amount of prejudice, hate, and wars. It's tough to envisage a world where corruption is eradicated and where unemployment, discrimination, and religious conflicts are non-existent, but that's the thing about hope — it can give us a positive charge even in the bleakest of times when our batteries are seemingly sucked dry.

Most of us don't have the power to create change on a big scale, but nobody stops us from giving our small part for the betterment of our existence on this planet. So even if you don't feel like your role is being felt, know that the truth is different because we all play small but crucial parts.

If we look for the brighter side of things, we will experience more positive events in our life, so don't give up hope. Stay driven and stay positive.

It's a Rap — Eminem Tribute

I would say I was a good kid, as I paid attention to what grown-ups were telling me most of the time. I listened to my mom for twenty-seven years; I listen to my dad to this day, and I have listened to Eminem for twenty years already. That's a pretty good stat Em has, as I have never met the guy.

Why am I mentioning these three people in the same breath? This may sound funny to you, but Eminem, a guy I consider to be a true poet, is a very influential person in my life, and the most important people I had while growing up — mom and dad — gave me the green light to listen to the lyrics I maybe wasn't supposed to when I was twelve or thirteen.

I still remember my sister raising the volume on our hi-fi system so I could hear "The Way I am" — a song that she considered to be pretty frickin' good. I kind of shrugged it off and pretended I was not impressed, but later I decided to re-listen to it and familiarize myself with some other songs from this artist. Soon enough, this blond, potty-mouthed rebel got under my skin, and even though I am a fan of many different artists, in general, I haven't looked back since.

So my dream and life's goal is to meet Eminem, and me mentioning this in my book seems logical to me. Let me explain why. Since these pages are the physical manifestation of my earlier goal, my idea was to incorporate this important wish on the very last page. I am not a superstitious person, but I kind of consider this a good juju.

Thank you, Eminem, for sharing your unparalleled gift with the world, for entertaining and inspiring millions, and for making me feel better thousands of times in my childhood and adult life. I even tidied up my English pronunciation by learning how to rap some of your songs from beginning to end.

So I hope… I know I will one day shake the hand you hold the pen in and squeeze the mic with "as you fight to the death."